STEWARDS OF GRACE

STEWARDS OF GRACE

By

DONALD COGGAN
Archbishop of York

" . . . as good stewards of the
manifold grace of God."

I Peter 4 [10]

London
HODDER & STOUGHTON

*Printed in Great Britain
for Hodder and Stoughton Ltd.
by Richard Clay and Company, Ltd.,
Bungay, Suffolk*

Dedicated
to
the clergy and lay readers
of the Diocese of Bradford—
my fellow-labourers in the Gospel of Jesus Christ.

I

A SPECIOUS LIE

"Our Father Below", so C. S. Lewis would have us believe, is subtle and insidious in his attack on the truth, and for that reason all the more difficult to controvert than if he were direct and open. If, therefore, he can insinuate, almost into the sub-conscious of present-day Christians, that the day of preaching is over, a major piece of strategy has been achieved. Preachers will go to their task as regularly as before—is it not ancient custom that from the pulpit, twice on Sunday, at least a few words should be spoken, probably attached, even if somewhat loosely, to a text? But they will go as men who have lost their battle before they start; the ground of conviction has slipped from under their feet.

The arguments behind the insinuation have enough in them to constitute a half-truth; and a half-truth is always an intangible thing with which to grapple. They run something after this fashion: A hundred years, even fifty years, ago the Church in any given community occupied a position which it can never occupy again. It was *the* centre not only of religion in the narrow sense of the term but also of the social life and entertainment of the people. Preaching, in days before radio and television exercised their kindly despotism, was something to be reckoned with, and great preachers had a listening (and often a reading) public which thought nothing of an hour's sermon—a sermon which was to be the subject of debate and of discussion till the next Sunday came round. Today the Church is no longer the centre of the community; wireless and television sets have taken the place of Bible and prayer-book in the living-rooms

of the average Englishman, and the Sunday paper has ousted
the re-print of the sermons of the great preachers which
used to find their way into thousands of homes. Further, the
argument runs, this is a headline age. The majority of our
people, for all the efforts of State education, do not *think*.
They scan. It is beyond their powers to follow a sustained
argument for, in so far as they read at all, they read little
more than the captions in the illustrated daily and weekly
periodicals, and, in so far as they listen in, they prefer the
news headlines to a closely reasoned lecture. Indeed, it
is true to say that many graduates of our Universities read
little but the journal of their own particular profession.

Modern man is bombarded, his ears by wireless and
gramophone, his eyes by television, poster and headline.
The result, paradoxically enough, is that he is fast losing the
capacity to hear (in the sense of listen) or to see (in the
sense of perceive). He is becoming the object of a fast-
moving series of visual and aural sensations. But the vast
majority of these sensations make little lasting impression on
him. They do not *register*. They pour off him, in the
common phrase, like water off a duck's back, leaving
him much the same as before, only a little less capable
of continued thought, of logical process, of reasoning.
Of what effect will preaching be in an age of men so
conditioned?

Again, the motor-car has constituted itself a major enemy
to preaching. "The week-end habit" militates against that
regular family Sunday worship which was one of the
characteristics of Victorian and Edwardian England. Modern
man, to use a phrase from the Prayer Book out of its context, "never continueth in one stay". He is in a state of
perpetual motion, though it must often be doubted whether
he knows where he is going. He has found the answer to
the question "How fast?", but he is far from finding the
answer to the question "Whither?" Is such a man capable

of sitting down and giving himself to the task of hearing the Word of God?

These arguments are true, obviously and demonstrably true—*so far as they go*. The trouble is that they do not go far enough or deep enough. And the conclusion drawn from them—that preaching is therefore of little value and its day is done—is, I believe, of diabolical origin and needs to be dealt with in the same way as all other suggestions which stem from the same source!

We need not waste time in elaborating the points which we have just made about contemporary English life, though we should think some long thoughts about the causes which give rise to them. (For example, is education, as it is now conceived, really nourishing, stimulating and preparing for life the young people committed to its charge, or is it simply cramming them with facts unrelated and ill-digested?) What we need to do is to go deeper and, in the light of the Christian revelation, ask some fundamental questions about the nature and destiny of the men and women who make up contemporary English life. In the light of the answers to these questions we may be able to judge of the relevance or irrelevance of preaching in this age. The following paragraphs are little more than out-linear, but if their argument is true they will leave little doubt as to the place which preaching should hold in the Church of the twentieth century.

Ours is a *frightened* world. It may well be that the noise and superficiality which characterize so much of our contemporary society and which prove so inimical to the work of the Church are the product of a fear which has gripped mankind. We "whistle to keep our courage up"; but down below the veneer of a care-free exterior there is the grip of a fear which is the child of uncertainty as to the meaning of life here and, if there is such a thing, of life hereafter. "Brave New World"—the old title rings hollow after two world wars and in the light, or rather, in the abysmal darkness, of the possibility of a third.

The astronomers have introduced us to a universe the size of which staggers us. Men today are often victims of what has been called "astronomical intimidation"—what do we count for in a universe of such stupendous proportions? Is it not realistic to think of ourselves as little more than insects, here today and gone tomorrow, liable to be crushed at any time by some chance heel, leaving behind us a fleeting memory and going into the unknown?

The physicists have unlocked for us sources of energy of which our fathers never dreamed—energy with vast potentialities for good, energy which in wrong hands may turn and rend us. Has modern man spiritual and ethical resources sufficient to enable him to use this energy aright? Or will he prove to have progressed technologically and regressed spiritually? Will he thus be like a child with a naked razor-blade in his hand, a mortal danger to himself and to those about him?

The State, which occupies so large a place in modern man's reckoning, is a benevolent monster. It provides us with education, pensions, health services and a dozen other benefits. But how easily can it become totalitarian, despotic, inhuman, treating men as ciphers in an age of automation; breeding a society which is increasingly de-personalized and in danger of becoming, in the words of Dr. F. R. Barry, the Bishop of Southwell, "a well-fed ant-hill"; breeding, indeed, a new kind of human being, all outside and no inside. Men become "hands" or even less, cogs in a vast impersonal State machine.

Small wonder, then, that man is frightened, oppressed by a sense of loneliness in a Universe which so often appears to be unfriendly and hostile. Gone are the days when his faith in Science (it was always right to spell it with a capital) was unshaken. Gone are the days when he believed

that Utopia was round the corner; given a little more knowledge and we should be there. There is a sense of dis-
illusionment among the more thoughtful members of
our society today which was lacking two or three decades
back. There is a humility among the greatest of our
scientists which is more than ready to admit that physical
science by itself does not begin to have all the answers.
Can it be that a place must be found for the Queen of
Sciences?

Frightened, lonely, disillusioned—strange adjectives to
use of men who outwardly are so confident, noisy, well-fed
and well cared for! And yet they are true. For man is restless till he finds his rest in God; ill at ease, till he finds,
with St. Augustine, that "in His Will is our peace"; home-
less and rootless till he comes home to the Family of God.
He is, in short, for all his achievements and his discoveries,
a sinner in need of the grace of God.

At this point we come to grips with the central facts of
the Christian faith. On the one hand, the sin of man; on
the other hand, the forgiveness of God. On the one hand,
the need of man; on the other, the provision of God. On
the one hand, the quest of man; on the other, the truth of
God. These things are the very stuff of which the Christian
revelation is made. But how are the forgiveness, the provision, the truth of God mediated to man in his sin and
need? This is a question of supreme importance. If in reply
we say "through the Word of God, incarnate, crucified,
risen, ascended", that is abundantly true. But it can only
provoke a further question, and it is this: "How does He
come to us, He whose earthly life was lived well-nigh two
thousand years ago, under conditions superficially so
different from our own?" To that question no single reply
can be given. Back of every reply must be the person and
work of the Holy Spirit, Lord and Life-Giver. But the
Spirit uses agents and instruments, and any reply would at

B

least have to include a reference to Bible, and to sacraments, and to human lives lived under the power of the Spirit and in the likeness of Jesus, and to preaching. A book could be written about each of these—indeed, libraries have been written about all of them. We, in this book, are concerned with the last, with preaching, and only with the others as they bear on preaching.

Here is the miracle of the divine economy, that between the forgiveness of God and the sin of man stands—*the preacher*! That between the provision of God and the need of man stands—*the preacher*! That between the truth of God and the quest of man stands—*the preacher*! It is his task to link human sin to forgiveness, human need to divine omnipotence, human search to divine revelation. The passage of time, the change in human conditions, the problems of "communication" do not change and cannot change these facts. They stand, so long as man is a sinner and so long as the grace of God is available for his need. "The gifts and calling of God are without repentance" (Romans 11²⁹) or, as J. B. Phillips puts it, "once they are made, God does not withdraw His gifts or His calling". Preaching is part of the divine plan so long as time shall last. The day of preaching is not over, precisely because God's grace and man's sin remain, and preaching is one of the mightiest links to join the two.

This is not to suggest that the *methods* used in preaching should not change. Far from it. New conditions call for creative thinking and daring experimentation in the difficult art of communication. All the wit of man and all the illumination of the Interpreter Spirit will be needed in conditions which are admittedly difficult and unprecedented. No longer can the Anglican shelter his homiletical nakedness behind "the beauty of our incomparable liturgy". No longer will a few thoughts hurriedly raked together on Saturday serve in place of a real ministry of the Word on

Sunday. *Anything* will not do, in a disillusioned, frightened, rootless generation.

The Editorial Notes of the first issue of *The Raven* (*A Bulletin on Expository Preaching*) began with these words: "About forty years ago, an Anglican writer declared that the day of the sermon was over. There is probably widespread agreement among preachers and congregations that the day of some sermons should be over. We think of the kind of sermon which aims at nothing in particular and hits it or the kind that is given to a discussion of modern problems and tempered with an oblique reference to the relevance of Christianity. If the sermon is the proclamation of the Gospel and if its unchanging background is to be found not in current events but in the Scriptures, the day of the sermon is not over. The sermon as thus conceived is part of the diet of Christian worship, for the primary meaning of Christian worship is nothing less than the setting forth in word and sacrament of the revelation of God in Jesus Christ." That is profoundly true.

There are not lacking indications today that, where there is a thoughtful, intelligent, prayerful, regular exposition of the Mind of God, in a form which shows the relevance of the Christian Faith to modern problems and needs, there is a hearing and a response. We do not pretend that the moment such a preacher enters his new Church, the crowds will flock to hear him. That is not true to life as it is today. We simply maintain that, given these provisos, it is a hard and glorious fact that a nucleus gathers, and generally increases, often to surprising proportions. For there is a hunger in the hearts of men, however blasé and self-satisfied they may appear to be—a hunger which can be satisfied with nothing less than the Word of the living God.

"Jesus came into Galilee, preaching . . ." (St. Mark 1¹⁴). No doubt people told Him that the times were not propitious for that kind of activity; that, apart from John the Baptist, the prophetic voice had been silenced for long, long decades; that men's minds were occupied with the hated invader and had no room for the things of God, and so on and so forth. The day of preaching was over! But Jesus had seen into the Heart of God, and He had seen, as had none other, into the heart of man. He was content if He might interpret the One to the other. So—"Jesus came preaching".

Is not that enough?

II

THE *ART* OF PREACHING?

THE heading of this chapter, apart from the question-mark,
is the title of a well-known book by Canon Charles Smyth
(S.P.C.K., 1940). The book has as a sub-title the words:
"A Practical Survey of Preaching in the Church of England
747–1939". To the use of the word *art* in that connection
not the slightest exception can be taken. But *in general*, can
preaching rightly be spoken of as an art? It is natural to
demur at the use of the word, for it smacks of human skill,
of human "polish" and achievement, and we feel that
preaching is something infinitely greater than this. So it is.
However we define preaching—and to this we shall give
some attention later—there must be in that definition some
element of the bringing together of the love of God and the
sin of man of which we spoke in the previous chapter. For
this, the word *art*, used in the sense of an unaided human
skill, seems too trivial, too lacking in the dimension of
eternity and of the numinous. Preaching throws the rope of
the Gospel to dying men—can this be called an art? Art
unaided has no converting power. All the gifts and tricks of
the orator are useless unless the preacher is in touch with
God, in love with men and on fire with the Gospel.
"Though I speak with the tongues of men and of angels
and have not love . . ." (1 Corinthians 13[1])—the warning
needs to be taken to heart.

And yet, if we constantly bear in mind this *caveat*, there
is a rightness about the use of the word *art* in connection
with preaching. Put the word in the company of its frequent
fellow, *craft*, and it takes on the right complexion. Dr.
W. E. Sangster, in a useful series of books, has accustomed

us to the use of the word craft: *The Craft of Sermon Illustration*
(1946); *The Craft of Sermon Construction* (1949); *Approach to
Preaching* (1952). One has heard the headmaster of a school
define the art of teaching as "the *strategy* by which we help
the child to develop". Art, craft, strategy—all these words
help in the conjuring up of a right conception of the
preacher's task. The New Testament describes followers
of the Christ as fishermen, shepherds, scholars. All these,
in their different ways, are strategists, bringing an art, a
skill, to bear on their work. As the preacher sits down at
his desk and rolls up the sleeves of his mind in preparation
for the ministry of the Word, he must say to himself: "I
am a strategist for my Lord, a craftsman at His task, an
artist at His work."

Yet how often the sermon fails to achieve its object not
because the preacher himself is not devoted, nor because
the theme is not great, but because his craftsmanship has
been clumsy or careless. He has shown no mastery of
strategy. "Your business", wrote Dr. James Black (*The
Mystery of Preaching*, p. 102) to would-be preachers, "is
serious gun-fire with a target." But only too often the
target is missed because of lack of attention given to the
weapon. "It will do, sir, won't it? It will do?" said the
student, as he waited during an ominous silence, on sub-
mitting a sermon to his College Principal. To which the
answer came, briefly but pointedly: "Do *what*?" So many
sermons *do* little, effect nothing great in matters of eternal
moment, because the art, the craftsmanship is faulty. They
meander like a harmless, babbling brook; they lack the
drive, the force, the power which more care to the detail of
strategy would bring them.

Behind that carelessness may well lie a lack of reverence
for the chief medium of our message. The carpenter uses
wood, the potter clay, the musician a piano or violin.
These are the media through which they work. The

preacher has but one medium, the medium of words. He may augment and enrich it by means of gesture, of inflection of voice, of flash of eye. But the stuff with which he works is words. Sacred things, they need handling with consummate care and with supreme reverence. They are, under the guidance of the Holy Spirit, bearers of the Word. "The Lord God", says the Servant of the Lord (Isaiah 50[4], Revised Standard Version), "has given me the tongue of those who are taught, that I may know how to sustain *with a word* him that is weary. Morning by morning he wakens, he wakens my ear to hear as those who are taught." That is a great ministry—to sustain him that is weary! And it is done "with a *word*". Modern totalitarian tyrants have proved the power of words—Hitler rallied a nation largely by the use of them. They are mighty weapons, for good or bad, if used with care and skill. "The words that I speak unto you, they are spirit and they are life" (St. John 6[63]). A study of the teaching of Jesus, and particularly of the parables, shows with what consummate skill He used the medium of words for the conveyance of divine truth. Of this I have written elsewhere (see my *The Ministry of the Word* (The Canterbury Press, 1945), p. 21). But here this must be added: If it be true that words are such sacred things, yes, and such dynamite, far more care will have to be given to the actual words employed in the delivery of our message than is often given today. It will not do to jot down a few headings and trust to the inspiration of the moment (or of the Spirit) to give us the right words at the time of delivery. To do that is to play into the hands of our own innate laziness; and God cannot honour that. How often, in his great war speeches, Winston Churchill drove his particular message home by the use of one striking (and perhaps unusual) word which he had chosen and prepared for that particular moment with the greatest care! Words can be as nails fastened in a sure place. We dare not trifle with them.

But it may be suspected that the ineffectiveness of many sermons has a deeper cause even than this. It is due to the fact that many preachers have not really wrestled with the fundamental question: "What is preaching?" It would be a wholesome discipline if the preacher could stop preaching for a week or two, and give the time which he would have devoted to sermon preparation to the answering of that question. He would do well to face it in the light of other subsidiary questions—What is the difference between a sermon and an essay? or between a sermon and a lecture delivered in a University or College?

It is not easy to define preaching, nor will it do to quote somewhat glibly the famous definition of Phillips Brooks, "the communication of truth by man to men" (*Lectures on Preaching*, p. 5), for it is patently inadequate. The chapter in which that definition occurs is a valuable one for the emphasis which it puts on two of the essential elements which must be present in any activity worthy of the name of preaching. But the definition raises a number of further questions. "Truth"—what kind of truth? And "by man" —what kind of man? Can *anyone* preach? If not, what are the essential qualifications which go to the making of a preacher, and without which he can only *talk*? And "to men"—does the preacher need some basic convictions about the nature and destiny of his audience? No: we must define our term far more carefully than this.

I do not propose to attempt to give a definition of preaching in this book. Rather, I would ask the reader, at this point or when he has finished reading this chapter, to make his own definition, to write it down, and to revise it a year hence, when he has had opportunity for further thought and prayer. It may be doubted whether an entirely satisfactory definition will ever be reached, for the simple reason that the activity of preaching is too vast to allow of short definition. But there are certain elements which must be included in any reasonably adequate definition of preaching, and I propose to hint at them by a series of quotations, sometimes with comment, sometimes without.

Let us begin with Bernard Lord Manning's definition. Preaching is "a manifestation of the Incarnate Word, from the Written Word, by the spoken word" (*A Layman in the Ministry* (Independent Press), p. 138). Certain inadequacies in this definition will at once be apparent (for example, what kind of man is to speak the word?) But it has the supreme merit of putting Christ, the Incarnate Word, right at the centre of preaching, and of anchoring preaching to the Written Word. Not all sermons will stand the test of the questions: "Do I manifest the Incarnate Word? Am I based on the Written Word?" Manning helps us to begin to move towards a definition of preaching.

We proceed. John Wesley, in his journal for July 17th, 1739, wrote: "I rode to Bradford five miles from Bath. Some persons had pitched on a convenient place, on the top of the hill under which the town lies. . . . There I offered Christ to about a thousand people, for wisdom, righteousness, sanctification and redemption." Again this does not give us a full definition of preaching. But it shows us Wesley the preacher "offering Christ" to men, standing between His wisdom and their folly, between His righteousness and their sinfulness, between His holiness and their defilement, between His redemption and their need, and *linking supply and need*. "I offered Christ." No wonder that Wesley defined his work as being that of "a man sent from God to persuade men to put Jesus Christ at the centre of their relationships". And must not the note of persuasion, and of volitional response, find some place in our definition of preaching?

Professor H. H. Farmer goes further and deeper than Phillips Brooks or John Wesley. "Preaching", he says (*The Servant of the Word*, pp. 27–28), "is that divine, saving activity in history, which began two thousand years ago in the advent of Christ and in His personal relationships with men and women, and has continued throughout the ages in the sphere of redeemed personal relationships (which is the true Church), now focusing on me, confronting me, as a person indissolubly bound up with other persons at this present time. . . . Preaching . . . is not merely *telling* me something. It is God actively probing me, challenging my will, calling on me for decision, offering me His succour, through the only medium which the nature of His purpose permits Him to use, the medium of a personal relationship.'' The passage is so stimulating that it is tempting to quote more. We note the element of volition, the probing of the will. And we note something lacking in the previous quotations, that preaching is a *divine* activity—''it is *God* probing . . . challenging . . . calling . . . offering''. This at once lifts preaching above the professional into the realm of the vocational.

St. Augustine has a sentence which we should bear in mind when working towards a definition of preaching. ''*Ita dicere debere eloquentem, ut doceat, ut delectat, ut flectat.*'' Which we may roughly translate: ''So ought the speaker to fulfil his task that he teaches, that he attracts, that he turns.'' That is to say, the appeal of his message must be to the whole man—to his mind (teaching), to his emotions (attraction), to his will (turning).

Our quotations so far have said little about the man who is God's agent in this His saving activity. But what we have said of the nature of preaching makes it abundantly clear that there are qualities demanded of the human agent which are not called for in an essayist or in a lecturer. Those qualities can be briefly summed up; he must be *a man of God* (on this see further Chapter Six). James Black was absolutely right when he said: ''Preaching is the natural overflow of our religion. We have received good news, and we long to tell it to others. . . . The reason and passion of preaching . . . is that a great and wonderful thing has come into our lives in the love of God through Jesus, and we can find no rest until we tell the world. . . . Preaching is telling someone else, one or many, about Jesus Christ, and opening out the mind and will of God'' (*The Mystery of Preaching*, pp. 20 and 21).

Is the reader ready to attempt a definition, albeit with trembling? Let him make sure of the centrality of Christ; let him see that his preaching is anchored to the Written Word; let him remember the element of persuasion and of volitional, as well as of mental and emotional, response; let him insist on the fact that preaching is a divine activity, and, moreover, that God, in the mystery of His wonderful economy, has entrusted it to His men.

> Through men whom worldlings count as fools,
> Chosen of God and not of man,
> Rear'd in Thy sacred training schools,
> Goes forward Thine eternal plan.

These are *some* of the ingredients necessary for inclusion in any adequate definition of preaching. It may be that the very defining may staunch the ineffectiveness which so often mars our work, and bring us back with renewed awe to the art, the craft, the strategy and, above all, the vocation of preaching. That vocation is nothing less than to show men, as the English merchant in Robert Wodrow's *Analecta* was shown during a visit to Scotland as he listened to three preachers there, ''the majesty of God; the loveliness of Christ; and all my heart.''

III

AN ARTIST AT WORK

THERE are three main ways of learning an art. *First*, there is the study of the literature which has grown up around it. In the case of preaching, this is very extensive indeed, and the writer of this series of essays is fully conscious of his temerity in adding to that literature. In a sense, preaching is founded on an ancient literature, the Bible. It is, as we saw in the last essay, "a manifestation of the Incarnate Word *from the Written Word*"; and it is to be doubted whether we should call that preaching which moves far from the revelation of God which is given to men in Holy Scripture. But in addition to the Bible, from which all true preaching springs, the literature of preaching includes volumes of sermons ancient and modern, and volumes about preaching. Here is indeed an *embarrassement de richesse*! We can never come to the end of the material provided for us.

Secondly, there is the actual doing of the thing itself. A would-be swimmer can read all the books in the library about swimming, but he will never become a swimmer till he jumps in! A painter can study the life and work of Leonardo da Vinci or of Picasso, but he will not become a painter till he takes up brushes and paints and goes to work! So it is with the preacher. All the theory in the world will not avail until, tremblingly and falteringly it may well be, he embarks on the task, and opens his mouth for his Lord. That is the way he will learn, and there can be no progress without it.

Thirdly, there is the study of the lives and work of those who, in some degree, have mastered the art before him.

This is a richly rewarding task. As the amateur violinist listens to Menuhin and watches the technique which over long years the great musician has mastered; as the would-be sculptor studies the works of Michael Angelo until in some degree the master's methods become his own; so the man who hopes to preach can learn an immense amount by studying the lives and methods of the great preachers whom God in His goodness has given to His Church in every age. Any bibliography of preaching should be rich in the biography of preachers. This is perhaps truer in the realm of preaching than in any other sphere, for in no "art" are artist and art so closely united as in the art of preaching.

In the wide realm of English preaching down the centuries few men have exercised so dominating an influence as Charles Simeon. It will repay us who aspire to be servants of the Word to study his life and work; and we shall devote the remainder of this essay to this task. More than a century has passed since his death, and mankind has moved on into a world utterly different from his. But the principles of life and work which lay behind his powerful ministry are of abiding value.

The life of Charles Simeon is so well known as to call for only the briefest summary here. Born in 1759, he was educated at Eton and then at King's College, Cambridge, of which he was a scholar and, later, Fellow. He was made deacon in 1782, and priest in the following year. That same year he preached for the first time at Holy Trinity Church, Cambridge, where he remained till his death in 1836. Thrice he was one of the deans of King's, its second bursar from 1798 to 1805, and its Vice-provost from 1790 to 1792. Of his share in the founding of the Church Missionary Society and of his support of the British and Foreign Bible Society nothing need here be said. Of his influence it must suffice to give two quotations, the first from Bishop Charles

Wordsworth (*Annals of my Early Life*, p. 335): Simeon "had a large following of young men—larger and not less devoted than that which followed Newman—and for a much longer time". The second quotation comprises the well-known words of Lord Macaulay, son of Zachary Macaulay, who was a friend of Simeon. He wrote, "As to Simeon, if you knew what his authority and influence were, and how they extended from Cambridge to the most remote corners of England, you would allow that his real sway over the Church was far greater than that of any Primate" (*Life of Lord Macaulay*, i. 67, note).

Few would dispute Simeon's right to a place even in a short list of great preachers. But wherein, precisely, lay his greatness as a preacher? The answer cannot be found simply in the length of his ministry in one place, remarkable though that was; nor in the strategic position which the incumbent of Holy Trinity Church, Cambridge, inevitably occupies; nor even in the immense volume of printed work which issued from his study, and which we have now in the twenty-one stout volumes of his *Horae Homileticae*, comprising 2,536 sermons, in regard to which Simeon at the end of his Preface wrote optimistically: ". . . if the Reader peruse *one discourse every day of his life*, the whole will occupy him exactly *seven years*." These facts, weighty though they are, do not go deep enough to explain his greatness.

For the sake of clarity and conciseness, we may suggest five factors which must be taken into consideration.

The *first* and most important factor was *the man himself*. Contemporary prints show us a man of obviously strong character, with prominent nose and determined chin. Indeed, for the major part of his life he fought a battle with his temper. But the portrait of him, taken at the age of forty-nine, which is now in King's College, and a reproduction of which serves as a frontispiece to H. C. G. Moule's

Life (1892 edition) shows a face marked by a combination of strength and sweetness which is singularly attractive and in part explains the extraordinary hold which he exercised over graduates and undergraduates, over "town" and "gown", for a long period of years. The circumstances of his conversion while an undergraduate at King's are well known. In that Passion Week of 1779, and especially on that Easter Sunday morning when he "awoke early with those words upon my heart and lips, 'Jesus Christ is risen today! Hallelujah! Hallelujah!' ", forces were liberated in Charles Simeon's soul which were never to cease operating till his death fifty-seven years later. Literally to his dying day he retained a sense of his deep unworthiness and of his utter indebtedness to the God who in Christ had redeemed him.

"No man who is too proud to be infinitely in debt will ever be a Christian." So J. S. Stewart has written (*A Man in Christ*, p. 224). This realization was the *fons et origo* of Simeon's greatness as a preacher. For it must be remembered that the sermon, as distinct from the lecture or the essay, consists quite as much in what the preacher *is* as in what he *says*. That is why preaching is so searching and humbling and sometimes terrifying a task.

The quality of his preaching was but a reflection of the quality of the man himself. And there can be little doubt that the man himself was largely made in the early morning hours which he devoted to private prayer and the devotional study of the Scriptures. It was his custom to rise at 4 a.m., light his own fire and then devote the first four hours of the day to communion with God. Such costly self-discipline made the preacher. That was primary. The making of the sermon was secondary and derivative.

The *second* factor was *the clarity of his aim*. Simeon in his Preface to the *Horae Homileticae* (I, xxi) writes: "The

Author . . . would wish his Work to be brought to this test—Does it uniformly tend

TO HUMBLE THE SINNER?

TO EXALT THE SAVIOUR?

TO PROMOTE HOLINESS?

If in one single instance it lose sight of any of these points, let it be condemned without mercy . . .'' That is strong language. But it cannot be denied that the possession of such an aim saves preaching from that "desultoriness" which characterizes so many so-called sermons which in actual fact consist of a few "nice thoughts" loosely strung together. Preachers of such sermons might have inscribed on their tomb-stones the lines:

> I shot an arrow into the air;
> It fell to earth I know not where.

Of Simeon this could never be said. He knew what he aimed at. Judging by the throngs which filled his church, by the scores of undergraduates who came week by week to his "conversation parties" in his drawing-room at King's, and by the world-wide influence of those who went out from Cambridge during his life-time to chaplaincies abroad and incumbencies at home, his sermons found their mark— sinners were humbled, the Saviour was exalted, holiness was promoted. Whatever language we in the twentieth century might prefer to use, it would be difficult to improve on Simeon's test of the main purpose of preaching.

The *third* was *the range of his themes*. By this I do not mean to suggest that the range of Simeon's sermon subjects was as encyclopaedic as is that of some twentieth-century preachers. (Parenthetically let it be hinted that this may not be so much a criticism of him as of those whose sermons seem but pale reflections of the news of the week, with a dash of religious flavouring!) What I wish to convey is that

c

Simeon refused to be cribbed, cabined and confined within the bounds of any system, be that system Calvinist or Arminian. He held too broad a view of Scripture to allow of that. "The Author is no friend to systematizers in Theology" (Preface to *Horae Homileticae*, I, xxiii). Nor would he confine himself simply to *doctrinal* preaching, vast as that subject is. With it he combined *ethical* preaching (*ibid.*, xxv). The theological climates of Simeon's day and of our own differ widely the one from the other. Nevertheless, one cannot but think that had his ministry been set in our own times there would have been much in the revival of Biblical theology of which he would have warmly approved, and not least in the "synthetic" approach to the Biblical doctrines which has ensued upon the "analytical" period, and in the emphasis on the double strand of *kerygma* and *didache*, to the appreciation of which C. H. Dodd gave such impetus in *The Apostolic Preaching and its Developments* (1936).

Simeon was happier in the atmosphere of "Both–And", rather than in the stuffier atmosphere of "Either–Or". One cannot refrain from quoting his famous dictum: "The truth is *not in the middle*, and *not in one extreme; but in both extremes*", a saying which Canon Charles Smyth describes as a grand discovery of Simeon's, "so naturally disconcerting to the English mind" (*Simeon and Church Order*, p. 185).

For half a century and more Simeon, to use his own words, was "content to sit as a *learner* at the feet of the holy Apostles", and "had no ambition to teach them how they ought to have spoken" (Preface to *Horae Homileticae*, I, xxiv). For fifty years and more, the main themes of his prayer and meditation were the great Biblical themes. It is this that accounts for the freshness which one still senses about the sermons of Simeon, however much one may doubt whether today they would have the effect that they had a century and a half ago.

The *fourth* factor was *the strength of his churchmanship*. No man with such an experience of personal conversion as Simeon had could fail to emphasize in his preaching and in his pastoral work the necessity of the individual's response to redeeming love. This Simeon constantly did, but never to the detriment of his emphasis on the corporate aspect of the faith. He was proud and glad to be a member of the Church of England. So Moule writes (*Charles Simeon*, pp. 259 and 260 and 108): "As regards the Church of England, his dearly beloved Mother Church, he has proved himself one of its truest servants and most effectual defenders. . . . He loved ancient order and solemn ordinances, and he magnified the office of the Christian ministry. . . . The Evangelical revival of the eighteenth century found a certain defect supplied in the school of Simeon. Its earlier leaders, with really few exceptions, were by no means careless of the essential sacredness of order and cohesion; but they found themselves often in circumstances where at least there seemed to be 'a need of disorder'. Simeon, one with them in main spiritual principles, always in quest, like them, of individual conversions, was led both by his situation and his reflections to a more distinct sense than most of them had felt of the claims of corporate and of national religious life. Never certainly did Simeon fail in loyalty to the objectivity, not only of the written Word of God, but of the historic Ministry and Sacraments." Such a sentence as the following, recorded by Canon A. W. Brown, is noteworthy: "In pronouncing it (the Benediction), I do not do it as a mere finale, but I feel that I am actually dispensing peace from God, and at God's command. I know not the individuals to whom my benediction is a blessing; but I know that I am the appointed instrument by whom God is conveying the blessing to those who are able to receive it" (*Recollections of Simeon's Conversation Parties*, p. 89).

No one who reads, for example, Simeon's four sermons on "The Excellency of the Liturgy" can fail to realize how profoundly his churchmanship affected his preaching (*Horae Homileticae*, II, Nos. 191–194, sermons preached before the University of Cambridge).

No review of Charles Simeon as a preacher can be allowed to conclude without a reference to a *fifth factor*—namely, *his revival of the formal sermon-scheme*. Canon Charles Smyth describes this as his "most noteworthy achievement" (*The Art of Preaching*, p. 178). Year in, year out, he expounded to successive generations of undergraduates the idea of a scheme or structural framework in the construction of the sermon. The twenty-one volumes of "skeletons" are the monument of Simeon's reintroduction of one of the main characteristics of medieval preaching. His fresh translation of Jean Claude's "Essay on the Composition of a Sermon", which forms the conclusion to the last volume of *Horae Homileticae*, shows his indebtedness to the seventeenth-century minister of the French Reformed Church at Charenton.

It cannot be doubted that this fifth factor, though in a sense a technical one relating more specifically to the *art* of preaching than do some of the former factors, was nevertheless one of great importance. Too many sermons, like the primeval chaos, are "without form and void". Simeon confessed that for the first seven of his preaching years "he did not know the head from the tail of a sermon" (A. W. Brown, *op. cit.*, p. 178). Until that at least is learnt, it may be doubted how much is achieved by homiletic meandering. "Preaching," wrote a great American preacher (H. S. Coffin, *What to Preach*, p. 155), "proposes to make men different." It is very difficult to achieve this aim if there be no clearly defined plan on the basis of which the sermon is built.

"If his *Horae Homileticae* are today as dead as a door-

nail", writes Canon Charles Smyth (*The Art of Preaching*,
p. 175), "the maxims which he inculcated at his Sermon
Parties on Friday evenings during Term are still exceedingly
alive." We would go farther. Simeon has something of
importance to say to the preacher of this age and of every
age, because the principles on which he based his preaching
are principles that a preacher of any age neglects at his
peril. The preacher of *every* age must take heed to himself,
to his aim, to the range of themes, to the strength of his
churchmanship and, not least, to the form in which he
couches what he has to say. When that is done, we may
look for a revival in our pulpit ministry.

IV
THE PREACHER AS TRUSTEE

It has been said that some men's sermons correspond to the Psalmist's description of the activity of the Almighty on a chilly day: "He casteth forth His ice like morsels: who is able to abide His frost?" There are, on the other hand, the sermons so often demanded by our friends across the Atlantic of those who visit their shores, sermons characterized by the adjective "inspirational". The late Henry Sloane Coffin once scathingly criticized the majority of such sermons as containing "a maximum of heat and a minimum of light"!

Have we not all listened to sermons which corresponded to both these categories? And have there not been times when we have preached such sermons? How are we to steer a middle course between the icy treatise suggested by the Psalmist and the empty verbosity described by Dr. Coffin?

I would affirm that the answer is to be found in a deep sense of our *trusteeship* as preachers.

Professor A. J. Gossip wrote a delightful *Appreciation* of W. M. MacGregor, which is printed at the beginning of the latter's Warrack Lectures for 1942–43, *The Making of a Preacher* (S.C.M. Press, 1945). He describes him as "not fiery-hearted and passionate, as the typical Gael is said to be, but notably calm and cool. . . . In speech he had no rushing spate of rapid oratory, but was among the quietest of speakers" (p. 8). Dr. Gossip continues: "This man was a preacher because he had heard incredibly good news which he could not keep to himself, but had to speak; because he knew Christ intimately, and exulted in this Friend of his of whom he was immeasurably proud. Not seldom during a sermon his face would break into a smile. Sometimes, I think, it was the artist's joy in the right phrase or the perfect quotation. But oftener it was sheer pride in the gospel that he was preaching, and in the Christ he was proclaiming, and in the wonderful God Whom he was seeking to reveal. It was indeed an irresistible Christ he preached, Who stormed the heart, whether one would or no. And, as one listened, how could one keep from wondering adoration of a God shown to be so adorable?" (*op. cit.*, p. 13). One cannot read this series of Warrack Lectures without being convinced that they came from one who knew himself to be a trustee.

This note of trusteeship sounds loud and clear in the pages of the Bible. The prophets are full of it, and their very vocabulary echoes it. Indeed, they are men bowed down with the weight of their conviction of trusteeship. Some message comes from the Lord to a prophet, and again and again it is described as a "burden". It is the identical word which is used of a load laid on an ass or mule or camel or hanging on a peg. So the prophet feels himself weighed down, until he has "delivered" the message with which he has been entrusted. Our modern phrase in which we speak of "getting a thing off one's chest" gives some idea of the notion of "burden" so familiar in the prophets.

Here is an Isaiah who, deeply conscious of personal and national sin, yet hearing the Voice which asks, "Whom shall I send, and who will go for us?", replies, "Here am I, send me." At once his offer of service is accepted. "Go, and tell . . ." He becomes a trustee of a message whose delivery will cost him more than he can realize. He is a man with a burden (Isaiah 6[8ff]).

Here is a Jeremiah. He is oppressed with a sense of diffidence, of youth, of inability as a speaker. Yet he hears the word of divine commission and encouragement—"thou shalt go to all that I shall send thee, and whatsoever I command thee thou shalt speak. Be not afraid of their faces; for I am with thee to deliver thee, saith the Lord" (Jeremiah 1^{6-8}). There are times in his ministry, indeed, when he rebels against the burden laid upon shoulders unaccustomed to so heavy a load. "O Lord, Thou has deceived me, and I let myself be deceived" (Jeremiah 20^{7ff}), he cries, with a frankness which would have been blasphemous if it had not been so utterly real. He determines to speak no more in God's name. But he cannot maintain such a spirit of rebellion. There is a fire in his bones to which he must give vent, or perish, and the fire is the word of God. He is a trustee.

Here is an Ezekiel, at one with his deported people in their misery by the canal Chebar, feeling the firm pressure of the Lord's hand upon him. "Son of man," comes the voice, "stand upon thy feet, and I will speak unto thee. . . . Son of man, I send thee . . . and thou shalt say unto them, Thus saith the Lord God. . . . And thou, son of man, be not afraid of them, neither be afraid of their words, though briars and thorns be with thee, and thou dost dwell among scorpions . . ." (Ezekiel 1^3, $2^{1, 3, 6}$). Such a message makes him a trustee.

Amos, very conscious of his country origin and of his "unclerical" background, a simple herdman and a gatherer of sycomore fruit, does not take upon himself the work of a prophet as a self-appointed task. With the solemn emphasis of a man with a burden entrusted to him he declares: "*The Lord* took me as I followed the flock, and *the Lord* said unto me, Go, prophecy unto my people Israel" (Amos $7^{14, 15}$).

Hosea, against the tragic background of a broken home-life and out of the bitterness of a broken heart, preaches the deep, pure love of God because he "can no other". He is a man with a burden. He cannot keep quiet, so long as men are spurning the divine compassion.

If the note of trusteeship is clear in the Old Testament,

how much clearer is it in the New, where the thing entrusted is so incomparably greater than it ever could be in the days before the coming of the incarnate Lord!

It is full and rich in the life and teaching of Jesus Himself. With a sure instinct, the writer of the Epistle to the Hebrews refers to Jesus as "the *Apostle* . . . of our profession" (Hebrews 3¹), for the sense of apostleship, of *sentness*, lies heavy on our Lord throughout His ministry. He is One who has received a divine commission. Hence the authority which astonished His hearers (St. Mark 1²²), and the urgency which marked His work and utterance. "I must be about My Father's business", so says the Lord not yet in His teens (St. Luke 2⁴⁹). "The Son of Man must be lifted up" (St. John 3¹⁴, cf. St. Mark 8³¹). "I must work the works of Him that sent Me, while it is day: the night cometh, when no man can work" (St. John 9⁴). "Other sheep I have, which are not of this fold: them also I must bring . . ." (St. John 10¹⁶). Sir Edwyn Hoskyns comments on this sense of necessity: "Normally in the Fourth Gospel the verb *it is necessary* denotes a divine requirement" (*The Fourth Gospel*, p. 252). Precisely so; this is the *burden* of the Lord. When, as the Cross drew near, our Lord handed back the trust to Him who had given it to Him, He could say: "I have finished the work which Thou gavest Me to do. . . . I have manifested Thy name unto the men which thou gavest Me. . . . I have given unto them the words which Thou gavest Me. . . . The glory which Thou gavest Me I have given them. . . . I have declared unto them Thy name. . . ." (St. John 17⁴, ⁶, ⁸, ²², ²⁶). Then, a little later, the great cry of triumph went up: "Finished!" (St. John 19³⁰). That was the restoration of a divinely imposed trust and task. Jesus could say, even more fully than the Psalmist before Him; "I have not concealed thy lovingkindness and thy truth from the great congregation" (Psalm 40¹⁰).

When we turn from the Gospels to the Epistles we find
the air still heavy with a sense of trusteeship. St. Paul has
caught the spirit of the Master. He is, indeed, an *apostle*.
There is a note of awed surprise about his remark: "We
were allowed of God to be put in trust with the Gospel"
(1 Thessalonians 2⁴). J. B. Phillips paraphrases that sentence: "We speak under the solemn sense of being entrusted by God with the Gospel." St. Paul "speaks . . .
in the Name of God, under the eyes of God, as Christ's
chosen minister" (2 Corinthians 2¹⁷, Phillips). So great
is his sense of wonder at the trust committed to him that he
has to coin a word (grammatically a monstrous concoction
of a superlative and a comparative combined) to express his
unworthiness—"to me whom am *less than the least* of all
saints was this grace given, to preach the trackless wealth
of Christ and to make all men see . . ." (Ephesians 3⁸).

The same emphasis recurs in the Pastoral Epistles.
Indeed, there is a word which comes thrice in the two
Epistles to Timothy, which occurs nowhere else in the
New Testament (1 Timothy 6²⁰; 2 Timothy 1¹², ¹⁴). It is
the noun *parathēkē*. The first and third occurrences of the
word are rendered by Moffatt as "the securities of the
faith", the second as "what I have put into His hands".
Arndt and Gingrich, in their great *Greek–English Lexicon of
the New Testament and Other Early Christian Literature*, translate
the word, "deposit, property entrusted to another". I
would suggest that the word has the same connotation in all
three passages. Thus in 1 Timothy 6²⁰, the writer charges
his son in the faith: "O Timothy, guard the deposit."
Similarly in 2 Timothy 1¹⁴: "Guard the splendid deposit
through the Holy Spirit who dwells in us." What of
2 Timothy 1¹²? I suggest: "I know whom I have trusted,
and am persuaded that He is able to guard the deposit
which is mine, till that Day." That is to say, God has
entrusted the writer with the sacred message of the Gospel,

a trust of shattering responsibility. But in His grace God
has not left him alone to guard so precious a treasure. He
himself will guard it. In fact, if we may dare to say so,
God and the writer are co-trustees. That means that the
burden is no longer intolerable; it is *shared*! Is not this part
of the meaning of "taking My yoke upon you"? (Further
references in the Pastoral Epistles to trusteeship may be
found in 1 Timothy 1¹¹—"the Gospel of the glory of the
blessed God, which was committed to me"; and in Titus 1³
—"God hath . . . manifested His Word through preaching
which was committed unto me.")

What *is* this *parathēkē*, this sacred deposit which Timothy
is charged to guard, and which the Apostle shares with His
Lord? What is it that has been committed to him, to keep
till the great Day? The context of the passages quoted
leaves us in no doubt. It is the Gospel, the Good News, the
story of the mighty Acts of God in Christ, the proclamation
that God, in mercy and grace, has visited and redeemed His
people.

Let it be repeated—for it needs to be, even at this hour
in the progress of theological thinking—that there is a
hemisphere of difference between God's Good News and
man's good views, however good the latter may be! For
Christianity is not primarily a new philosophy but a divine
rescue operation.

On his return from a visit to America, Canon Alec
Vidler wrote in *Theology* (February 1948, Vol. LI, p. 45):
"So far as I can ascertain, the paradigm of American
preaching is: 'Let me suggest that you try to be good.'
Moralistic homilies are still the order of the day. They are
delivered, no doubt, with various degrees of eloquence,
and they may recommend various degrees and forms of
virtue or piety. There may even be such preachers with
fire in their bellies, though I have not come across them."
Canon Vidler accused them of "not exposing the basic

human predicament, namely, that the attempt to justify ourselves by good works inflates our pride so that our progress in health turns into a worse disease. This predicament being unrealized, there is blindness to the starting-point of the Gospel of the New Covenant. You are still preaching the Law, and a pretty easy-going or romantic Law at that.''

One is reminded of Richard Niebuhr's satire of a certain type of preaching: ''A God without wrath brought men without sin into a Kingdom without judgment through the ministrations of a Christ without a Cross.'' Niebuhr presumably had American preaching chiefly in mind. But such a parody of preaching is by no means entirely confined to America. Canon C. C. Smyth, in a memorable essay (*The Church of England in History and Today* in *The Genius of the Church of England*, p. 35; S.P.C.K., 1947), recalls how the three folio volumes of Archbishop Tillotson's sermons on the Gospel of Right Conduct grafted imperishably on the English mind the sense of duty. So effective were they that ''it was necessary for the Methodists and Evangelicals to revive the doctrine of Redemption, and for the Oxford Movement to recover the doctrine of the Church''. He continued: ''The Gospel of Right Conduct is perilously akin to the convention of Good Form; and the trouble with an ethical morality is that it is so easily, if not safely, detached from its doctrinal sanctions and boiled down to 'being good and making people happy'. A French observer has lately said that 'England remains a Christian country chiefly in an ethical sense'.'' That observation raises the question as to how long Christian ethics will persist if divorced from Christian doctrine. The New Testament would seem to suggest very strongly that Christian conduct is the direct outcome of Christian belief. The Christian *parathēkē*, the Christian Gospel, precedes all codes of Christian conduct, as indeed it is the life-spring of them all.

This fact of a sacred deposit of truth committed to the preacher has as its logical consequence two corollaries, corollaries which superficially appear to be contradictory but which will easily be seen to be complementary.

(i) *The Christian preacher has a boundary set for him.* When he enters the pulpit he is not an entirely free man. There is a very real sense in which it may be said of him that the Almighty has set him his bounds that he shall not pass. He is not at liberty to invent or choose his message: it has been committed to him, and it is for him to declare, expound and commend it to his hearers. He is in the position of St. Paul, who wrote to the Corinthians that he "delivered . . . that which he also had received, how that Christ died for our sins according to the Scriptures, and that He was buried, and that He rose again the third day according to the Scriptures, and that He was seen . . ." (1 Corinthians 15$^{3-5}$). *That*—was it the original Damascus creed which he "received" immediately after his conversion?—that was the framework of the sacred deposit, of the Gospel; and woe betide him if he preaches "another Gospel which is not another" (Galatians 1$^{6, 7}$). "Woe is me if I preach not the Gospel" (1 Corinthians 9^{16}) does not only mean "Woe is me if I am silent when I should speak", but also "Woe is me if I do not faithfully deliver that which is committed unto me in trust, committed to me by my Lord until that Day". There is a boundary set for the preacher, a boundary which marks him off for ever from the historian or essayist. *In a sense*, their fields of operations are wider than his. They have no divinely appointed bounds which they may not pass. It is reliably reported that in 1955 a course of Lenten orations was delivered from a pulpit in the South of England entitled "The Difficulties of the Church of England in the Reign of Charles II". They could scarcely be called a course of *sermons preached*.

(ii) *The Christian preacher has well-nigh boundless scope.* His

theme is as wide, as far-reaching, as pervasive as the grace
of God. His traffick is with "the many-coloured, variegated
wisdom of God" (Ephesians 3^{10}). He deals with "the
many-splendoured thing". His task is to hold up the jewel
of God's truth to catch as many lights as may be, that all
may see its glory. Not for him contentment with one facet
of the truth, however great that facet may be. Not for him
some theological or religious bee in the bonnet, some
groove which so easily can become a grave for himself and
his people!

There is a moving story in the Acts of the Apostles (Acts
20^{17ff}) which tells of how St. Paul bade farewell at Miletus
to the elders of the Church at Ephesus. He had spent
longer at that place than at any other in the whole of his
recorded evangelistic ministry. Public ministry had gone
together with house-to-house visitation. At the end of his
service there he was in a position to declare that he had
kept back nothing that was profitable to them, and that he
had "not shunned to declare unto them the whole counsel
of God". *The whole counsel of God*—that is enough to stretch
any man, and to last him to a very old age!

There is something infinitely exhilarating about this. The
greatest preacher in the world, as he stands before the
immensity of the everlasting Gospel, must feel like a little
child, bucket in hand, attempting to scoop up the Atlantic
Ocean! How can he compass such a task? He cannot.
But he can keep at it, at once refreshed by its glory and
awed by its immensity, until the day when he shall know as
he has been known.

There is a fine passage in Arthur Porritt's *Life* of Dr.
J. H. Jowett (Hodder & Stoughton, pp. 217ff.) in which the
writer tells us that for the great preacher redeeming grace
was "the 'big theme' to which, above all others, he returned again and again, as if, of all truth, it was the one
facet that entranced him". He saw it as the theme regnant

of all Christian theology. It fascinated him, and held him within its grip. "In a hundred sermons he proclaimed it. All his wealth of imagery and illustration was lavished upon this theme. . . . He was always probing into the depths of its meaning and discovering some new aspect of its unsearchable riches."

It is a great thing to come under the magnificent tyranny of the Gospel! For a tyranny it is, though the tyranny of love. The burden imposed on the preacher is a heavy one, nor are its demands relaxed as life goes on.

There is the demand, for example, of *study*. When the archdeacon or his deputy presents those to be admitted Deacons or Priests he is bidden by the Bishop to "take heed that the persons, whom ye present unto us, be apt and meet, *for their learning* and godly conversation, to exercise their ministry duly . . ." That does not mean that all the candidates must be budding Doctors of Divinity (though it is much to be desired that the proportion of graduates among ordinands were considerably higher than it is today). It does mean that they are to be men "studious . . . in reading and learning the Scriptures", men who, "by daily reading and weighing of the Scriptures, . . . wax riper and stronger in their ministry". The Church of England expects its clergy to be not only "discreet" but also "learned" ministers of God's Word. When the Bishop tells the candidates that "ye ought to forsake and set aside (as much as you may) all worldly cares and studies", he is, of course, warning them against that worldliness which is the snare of every ministry, and against that dissipation of energy which would not allow them to say, with St. Paul, "this *one* thing I do" (Philippians 3^{13}). But the Bishop is doing more. He is bidding them get their priorities right—not, indeed, that they should be men of one book only, but that they should draw all their "cares and studies *this way*".

When that wise leader of men, Oswald Chambers, was

seeking to help a man who found himself in a mental cul-de-sac, Chambers asked him what he read. He replied that he read nothing but the Bible and books directly associated with it. Chambers replied: "The trouble is you have allowed part of your brain to stagnate for want of use", and forthwith proceeded to give his friend a list of over fifty books, philosophical, psychological, theological, covering almost every phase of current thought. The result was a revolution which could only be described as a mental new birth. Chambers wrote later to his friend: "When people refer to a man as 'a man of one book', meaning the Bible, he is generally found to be a man of multitudinous books, which simply isolates the one book to its proper grandeur. The man who reads only the Bible does not, as a rule, know it or human life" (*Oswald Chambers: His Life and Work*, p. 133). That is the meaning of drawing all our cares and studies *this way*.

There is, again, the demand for the *enquiring mind*. Too many preachers have lost, if they ever had it, a sense of wonder, of awed surprise at the magnificence of nature as well as of revelation. Wonder gets us close to worship. A lack of a sense of wonder narrows and cramps a man's preaching and ministry. Tennyson knew the meaning of wonder—

> Flower in the crannied wall,
>   I pluck you out of the crannies,
> I hold you here, root and all, in my hand,
>   Little flower—but *if* I could understand
> What you are, root and all, and all in all,
>   I should know what God and man is.

Let the man who has lost his sense of wonder, whose horizons have shrunk, whose mind has ceased to enquire, read Charles E. Raven's Gifford Lectures for 1952, *Natural Religion and Christian Theology* (Cambridge University Press,

D

2 vols., 1953). Whether or not he finds himself able to subscribe to the theology of these volumes, he will be a strange man if his sense of wonder is not re-kindled by the reading of them.

It is a fact well known to students of the Fourth Gospel that the writer studiously avoids, throughout the book, the use of the nouns "belief" and "knowledge". Reasons have been sought for this strange phenomenon, all the stranger because the corresponding verbs are so frequent in their occurrence. One theory, in itself quite probable, is that the nouns were used in current literature of a Gnostic or semi-gnostic character, and that the Evangelist did not wish to use words which were so "tainted". R. H. Lightfoot posits another reason. He writes that the Evangelist, by the very avoidance of the use of these nouns, "indirectly, but unmistakably, emphasizes that the religious belief which is set forth in this Gospel, and to engender which he wrote it, is no passive or unchanging state, still less a formal adherence to a set of propositions: it is a life of energy and growth, in which, although the end is implicit in the beginning, there is always more in front of the believer than he has been granted, or has been able as yet to make his own; and in this process, which is throughout a matter of believing, knowledge itself can never dare to cease to learn; from time to time it dies to live" (*St. John's Gospel: A Commentary*, Oxford University Press, p. 25). If this is true, and I believe it to be abundantly so, the demand for an enquiring mind is rooted in New Testament theology.

Yet again, and lastly, there is the demand for *intellectual honesty*. "For me", writes Canon Charles Smyth in the essay referred to above (in *The Genius of the Church of England*, p. 42), "the historic hall-mark of the piety of the Church of England is a stubborn intellectual integrity. I have noted this particularly in regard to Laud and Maurice, though it runs through all I have been saying, and Mandell Creighton, a

great ecclesiastical historian and the first bishop with a
modern mind, was an illustrious example of it.'' It certainly is a demand, a searching demand, made on the
preacher who is a trustee of the Gospel. This does not
mean that the preacher is to make the pulpit the arena in
which he wrestles with his doubts and intellectual problems.
The study is the place for that activity. It is more important
to declare than to debate in the pulpit. But it should at
least be apparent to the intelligent listener that he who
occupies the pulpit is not unaware of the movements of
thought of the century in which he lives, and that he has at
least glimpsed the bearing of the everlasting Gospel on
contemporary problems and needs. The Old Testament
prophets had an uncanny way of stating timeless truth, but
that statement of truth was always made in direct relation
to some burning issue of the day. There was a fearless
honesty, a pointed relevance, to their every utterance.

We have already referred, in this chapter, to the
Ordinal. Let me close with a further reference to it.
When a man is made deacon, the Bishop delivers to him a
New Testament, saying, ''Take thou authority to read the
Gospel in the Church of God, and to preach the same . . .''
When he is made priest, the Bishop delivers to him ''kneel-
ing, the Bible into his hand, saying, 'Take thou authority to
preach the Word of God, and to minister the holy Sacraments . . .' '' When a priest is made a Bishop, the Archbishop delivers him a Bible, saying, ''Give heed unto
reading, exhortation and doctrine. Think upon the things
contained in this Book. Be diligent in them . . .'' Here is
symbolism pregnant with meaning. Thus the sacred trust is
handed over and handed on from age to age. Nothing other
than the Bible is put into the candidate's hand. It is for him
to hold the Christian deposit, to grasp it ever more firmly
and to expound it ever more faithfully.

V

THE PREACHER AS INTERPRETER

"CRIST and His apostlis taughten ye puple in yat tunge yat was moost knowun to ye puple. Why shulden not men now do so?" So wrote John Wycliffe. He conceived it to be his God-given task to make the message of God, as contained in the Bible, available to the "man in the street". It is interesting that of the copies of the Wycliffe Bible which are now extant many are small, unadorned and closely written. This is an indication that they were intended, not for the great nor for institutions, though there were copies for such, but for the ordinary reader. "Assisted by some of his followers . . ., the whole Bible was translated into English during the last few years of Wycliffe's life, and copies soon began to circulate. This stupendous task, carried out in the teeth of considerable opposition and danger, represents Wycliffe's greatest work for the Church" (J. R. H. Moorman, *A History of the Church in England*, p. 121). It was an achievement all the more remarkable when it is remembered that the first Wycliffe Bible (1382) appeared more than a century and a half before the death of William Tindale (d. 1536) and nearly two centuries before that of Miles Coverdale (d. 1568). The worthy Thomas Fuller pondered on the action of Fleming, Bishop of Lincoln, who, in 1428 under orders from Pope Martin V, exhumed and burnt the bones of Wycliffe and scattered his ashes on the River Swift. He wrote: "This brook hath conveyed his ashes into Avon; Avon into Severn; Severn into the narrow seas; they into the main ocean. And thus the ashes of Wycliffe are the emblem of his doctrine, which now is dispersed all the world over"

(*The Church-History of Britain*, Book IV, sec. ii, par. 53, p. 171).

The courageous action of Wycliffe in the fourteenth century is a challenge to the preacher of the twentieth. It is not indeed our task to translate from Latin into English, but it is our task to preach in a "language understanded of the people". It is much to be feared that, only too often, we do *not* use "yat tunge . . . moost knowun to ye puple", but rather a jargon understanded, perhaps, by the philosopher or the theologian, but far too complicated and technical for the wayfaring man or indeed for the man whose profession or skill is other than our own.

It may readily be admitted that the atmosphere of the day is conducive to the use of jargon. As knowledge advances, learning becomes increasingly specialized, until we are in danger of producing a race of specialists who, in the words of the well-known definition, "know more and more about less and less until they know everything about nothing at all". The average layman cannot begin to understand the language of a scientific text-book—it is technical to a degree. Probably there is not much that can be done about the difficulty. If a particular branch of science is to be mastered, or even understood in the outskirts of its ways, the language of that science must be learnt, and there are no two ways about it. Nevertheless, the matter is giving concern to the scientists themselves. Sir Raymond Priestley, President of the British Association in 1956, said that he himself found a good deal of science unintelligible, and declared war on scientific jargon. He maintained that the young scientist frequently used jargon because clothing his thoughts in simple words required an effort which he was not prepared to make. That charge applies to others besides scientists!

But there is another kind of jargon which affects us today. It is the English (if we may dignify it by that name) beloved

of Government forms, pronouncements, edicts. Not the
least of the factors which made the English of the 1611
version of our Bible and of Coverdale so incomparably
lovely was their use of simple, and often of monosyllabic,
language. Listen to this, for example: "O God, thou art
my God; early will I seek thee: my soul thirsteth for thee,
my flesh longeth for thee in a dry and thirsty land, where
no water is. . . . Thus will I bless thee while I live: I will
lift up my hands in thy name" (Psalm 63$^{1, 4}$). Or again:
"For lo, the winter is past, the rain is over and gone; the
flowers appear on the earth; the time of the singing of
birds is come, and the voice of the turtle is heard in our
land" (The Song of Solomon 2$^{11, 12}$). Shakespeare knew the
power of monosyllabic simplicity. Listen to this:

> So we'll live,
> And pray, and sing, and tell old tales, and laugh
> At gilded butterflies, and hear poor rogues
> Talk of court news; and we'll talk with them too,
> Who loses and who wins; who's in, who's out;
> And take upon 's the mystery of things,
> As if we were God's spies.
>
> *King Lear*, Act V, Scene 3.

But modern jargon, journalese, the language of Government circulars, is not content with the beauty—and the
power—of simplicity. George Orwell has parodied the
tendency which we are deploring. He takes a well-known
verse from Ecclesiastes (9^{11}), which in the Authorized
Version runs as follows: "I returned and saw under the sun
that the race is not to the swift, nor the battle to the strong,
neither yet bread to the wise, nor yet riches to men of
understanding, nor yet favour to men of skill; but time and
chance happeneth to them all." Then he gives it to us in
modern English: "Objective consideration of temporary

phenomena compels the conclusion that success or failure in competitive activities exhibits no tendency to be commensurate with innate capacity, but that a considerable element of the unpredictable must invariably be taken into account" (in *Politics and the English Language*, one of the essays in *Shooting an Elephant and Other Essays* (Secker & Warburg, 1950), p. 92). It was only the regulations of Parliamentary procedure which made Winston Churchill say that an opponent had indulged in a "terminological inexactitude". He would much rather have said a "lie", and thus saved ten syllables! He has been a consistent opponent of officialese and of that laborious use of English which is so poor a substitute for the simple and often the monosyllabic. His references to Hitler as "that bad man" sounded in our ears like the report of a machine-gun during the years of the last war.

It would be all to the good if a campaign were waged for simplicity of language in preaching. Preachers might well be encouraged to read Sir Ernest Gowers' *Plain Words: A Guide to the Use of English* (H.M. Stationery Office, London, 1948) and *An A.B.C. of Plain Words*. They would find these books practical and amusing. We are not pleading for the childish, still less for the undignified. The preacher is an ambassador. A simple dignity befits his message. He will be very cautious, for example, about the use of slang. He will probably use it only on the rarest occasions when the use of some current popular phrase *says* something which otherwise could not be expressed except by some clumsy circumlocution. He holds the priceless treasure of the Gospel. He will not present the pearl of great price to the people wrapped up, as it were, in newspaper. His wording and phraseology will be a worthy casket for the treasure. Polonius' advice to his son is as applicable to preachers as to travellers: "Be thou familiar, but by no means vulgar" (*Hamlet*, Act I, Scene 3). The preacher who seeks to be a

worthy craftsman will be mindful of the words of Dr.
W. R. Maltby, who, when writing of "A Preacher's
Damnation", said: "He spoke of great things and made
them small; of holy things and made them common; of God
and made Him of no account."

Language matters. It is our medium when we are seeking
to translate the things of God so that they may be understood by our people. Bishop Henry Compton, who for
thirty-eight years was Bishop of London (1675–1713) and
who proved himself a father in God to his clergy and people,
warned his clergy that they must "weigh well what they are
going to do, for it is not little Harangues sprinkled with
Philosophy that will do the Business they come about". In
preaching, they must make themselves understood. "They
ought to suit the harangue to their Auditors, to express
themselves in as plain familiar Terms as possible and use
Expressions for edification of the Mind and not to tickle
the Ear" (quoted in Edward Carpenter, *The Protestant
Bishop: Being the Life of Henry Compton, 1632–1713, Bishop
of London* (Longmans, Green & Co., 1956), p. 211). That
is well said.

But the problem of communicating the truth of the
Christian revelation to our contemporaries goes much
deeper than the level of the precise English vocabulary
which we use. The matter of *idiom* calls for considerable
care. The Bible is entirely an Oriental book. Much of its
idiom and imagery is entirely foreign to the Western mind.
This did not matter so much when the Bible was practically
the only book read in the home, and when it was pondered
and explained to the child almost from the cradle. But, in
these days when the Bible has been dethroned from its
place of authority and familiarity in home and school, its
imagery is strange and unfamiliar. A simple and, perhaps,
extreme illustration will serve to make the point clear.
I take it from the life of that remarkable man, Dr. John

Stansfeld, whose work in the East End of London influenced William Temple and a host of others:

"A junior officer (of the Oxford and Bermondsey Club) chose for his text 'Two sparrows for a farthing'.

" 'Sparrers?' he began on a note of derision. 'We don't sell no sparrers, not in Bermondsey. *Kippers* is what 'E would 'ave said if 'E'd been 'ere. A pair of Kippers sold for three-'aipence—*that's* wot 'E meant.' In a few more sentences he compared the worth of the least of Club members with even the best kippers, and a dark corner of the Gospel was immediately flooded with a bright light" (*The Doctor: The Story of John Stansfeld of Oxford and Bermondsey*, by Barclay Baron (Edward Arnold, 1952), p. 24).

I doubt whether that address was quickly forgotten by those who heard it. That junior officer in Bermondsey showed real imagination in translating Eastern idiom into Western. In a very real sense he was a follower of the Master, Who, before *giving* the bread to the disciples, *broke* it. *O si sic omnes!*

So far in this chapter we have cast a glance at the twin problems of vocabulary and of idiom with which any preacher must wrestle, and constantly wrestle, if he is to translate the Gospel. But we have not gone deep enough, not by a very long way. For, if we are to be the means by which the Gospel "comes alive" to the twentieth-century man, we must seek to understand the mental and psychological climate by which he is conditioned.

A conversation that I had, some years ago, with Dr. Welch, then head of the religious department of the British Broadcasting Corporation, often comes back to my mind. "I wish", he said to me in effect, "that in Theological Colleges, where so great attention is given (and rightly) to the seed, more attention were given to the soil in which the seed of the Word of God is to be sown." He spoke against a background of considerable study in anthropology and of years spent in the peculiarly difficult and delicate work of religious broadcasting. In reply, I reminded him that the so-called Parable of the Sower is really the Parable of the Soils. In it, our Lord is not concerned with the sower of the seed, except in passing, but He focuses His attention and ours on the different kinds of soil into which the seed falls.

The word of God never comes to men in a vacuum; it is always conditioned by the circumstances and by the subtle "atmosphere" of the life of the day. Consider the following list: the invention of the steam-engine, the Industrial Revolution, the abolition of the slave-trade, the discovery of anaesthetics, of the telephone, cinema, wireless and television, the use of aerial transport and warfare and of atomic energy, the researches of such men as Eddington and Jeans and the writings of Fred Hoyle on the nature and structure of our universe, the rise and development of biblical criticism and of the study of comparative religions— a mixed and varied list. Not one of those things would have had any meaning for a reader two hundred years ago. More has happened in those two centuries—perhaps we might safely say in the last century—than in all the previous years of the Christian era. Man's whole life and outlook have been revolutionized by these things. It is true, indeed, that the seed is the same as it was in 1758, but the soil is entirely different. We must come to terms with this fact; if we do not, we may speak with the wisdom of a Solomon and the eloquence of a Chrysostom, but we shall not speak *to our age*—the seed will fall beside the way.

Before a doctor can prescribe, he must diagnose. Before we in our day can be evangelists and physicians of the soul, ministering effectively "the wholesome medicines of the doctrine" of the Gospel, we must consider the patient, the diseases of whose soul we are out to heal. What is his outlook on life? Viewing religion through his eyes, we enquire: How does he see it? For the sake of brevity and ease of reference, we will call him Tom. He is a normal twentieth-century young man, let us say in his thirties or forties. If we make the following assertions about him, we shall not be far off the mark.

(i) *For Tom the Bible lacks authority.* His grandfather, though probably not his father, was content to live life in such and such a way "because the Bible said so". Symbolic of this attitude was the place which the Bible occupied on a central table in the drawing-room. It was enthroned there. Nothing was allowed on top of it. But it is thus enthroned no longer. In Tom's parlour the central place is given to the *Radio Times* or to *John Bull* or to *Reveille* or, if he is made that way, to Dylan Thomas. To say to him, "You must believe this, or live life in this way, because the Bible says so", does not ring a bell. We wish it did. But that does not alter the fact that it does not.

(ii) *Tom suspects that Christianity is narrow and confined in its origins and relevance.* He connects it (as a matter of fact correctly) with a particular *people*, the Jews (whom he dislikes). He connects it (as a matter of fact one-seventh correctly) with a particular *day*, Sunday, which for him quite possibly has negative and prohibitionary associations. He connects it with a particular and rather remote and intangible part of him, his so-called "soul". He, like all the rest of the people with whom he works, plays and goes to the cinema, has very real problems connected with sex, and love, and money, and (increasingly) leisure. "But", he asks, "has Christianity in 1958 anything to say about *that* kind of thing?"

(iii) *Tom suspects that Christianity*, concerned with beliefs about whose credibility and relevance he has many doubts, *is not very concerned with social problems.* Sir Oliver Lodge got hold of a dangerous half-truth when he said that modern man is not worried about his sins. (We may contrast G. K.

Chesterton, who, on being asked why he was joining the Roman Catholic Church, replied, "To get rid of my sins.") But whatever the truth may be about this question, Tom and his generation *are* concerned about social wrong and about the obvious disease of the whole social order. He wants to know whether Christianity has a word to say about this. Or is he to think that secular Socialism alone is concerned with these things?

(iv) *Tom is vaguely aware of other faiths.* He saw them, though often at a distance, during the time of his National Service. He read about them in the newspapers, or maybe he even side-glanced at comparative religion in his study of history at the university or at evening classes. His own faith being very thin and second- or third-hand, he is inclined to maintain that these other religions are only different versions of the same thing, and we shall all arrive at the same place in the end. He is not quite sure whether that is annihilation or that queer kind of state where a Heavenly Grandfather reigns who would not hurt a fly and whose only wish it is that a good time should be had by all; but we are all going in the same direction, though perhaps by different routes.

(v) *Tom thinks "scientifically" rather than Biblically.* (The verb perhaps makes too great a claim, for much modern education does not produce thinking at all. The first adverb is used in the modern sense, which forgets what Spenser referred to as "The Queen of the Sciences" and uses the term as referring only to the physical sciences.) He thinks secularly rather than Scripturally. He is at home with test-tubes but uncomfortable with the Psalms. Speak to him (if you can!) of hydrogen, of valves, amplifiers, coils and frequency and he is on his own ground. Speak to him of salvation, of justification, sanctification and grace, and he is lost. Do not *blame* him for this. Do not shake your head and lament for the good old days. Get to grips with the *fact.* It goes very deep. It goes back to the *home*, where his grandfather went to church but his father and mother did not (with all the suggestion that is thus made on a child's mind that Christianity is out-dated and only for the old folks.) It goes back to the *school*, where the science laboratory with its apparatus and explosions was much more vivid and ''real'' than the Scripture lesson (if he had one), which, often as not, was taught by an unconvinced, if not unbelieving or unintelligent, teacher. It goes back to the *university*, where the whole approach to history, science, ethics and so forth was more than likely secular in its atmosphere. He tends to equate the adjective ''old'' with the adjective ''out-dated'', and his very superficial acquaintance with Bible and prayer-book corroborates the equation in his thinking.

If this is not a totally false analysis of Tom's outlook, if it is a fairly sound appraisal of the intellectual ''climate'' of his day, the preacher is faced with a problem of vast proportions and extreme delicacy. He dares not ignore what we have just been discussing. If he does, he will soon find himself preaching to a tiny handful of the elect whose average age is immense and whose funerals occur with alarmingly rapid frequency. He believes that in the Bible we have the record of God's revelation of Himself to man in his sin and need. He believes that the Spirit breathes upon the Word and brings its truth to light, making it a living Word of God to men. He believes this because the Spirit has done it (and continues to do it) for him, and because the history of the Church records that He has done it down the ages. This he believes. If he did not, he would cease to preach. But believing it with all his heart, he longs to become increasingly an expository preacher, to unloose and apply the healing power of the Word of God to Tom and the likes of Tom.

How is he to approach his task? I have no ''pat'' answer

to a question of such complexity, no panacea for the sickness of an age hard of hearing to the Voice which is always seeking to make itself heard to *homo viator*. But perhaps certain lines of approach may be sketched, suggested by the very assertions about Tom and his mental outlook which we made earlier in this chapter.

(1) If it is true that the Bible lacks authority for him, perhaps we should invert our method of approach. If the "Thus saith the Lord" which Tom's grandfather found authoritative for him is so no longer, we must begin elsewhere and work towards that point where we can say, "But the Bible said so all along." We must work on that great principle of teaching whereby the teacher begins with the known and works towards the unknown. The unknown, in this case, is the Bible. He must start from facts which he can see and with which he is familiar, start from life and work towards the Biblical revelation. Let me illustrate.

Tom knows full well that one of the symptoms of our day is the recurrence, in all ranks of life, of nervous breakdowns. His newspapers and friends tell him that our mental hospitals and institutions are full. That is a fact which he cannot evade. Cannot the expository preacher begin *there*, and work from that undeniable fact towards the Biblical view, which holds that, if a man lives his life without God at the centre, he is *eccentric* ("O God, Thou hast made us for Thyself, and we are restless till we find our rest in Thee")? On the basis of twentieth-century statistics, he may expound the Biblical meaning of peace and reconciliation and the Biblical doctrine of man.

Tom knows (did he not serve in the Forces?) of the incidence of venereal disease and of its consequences. Can we not, beginning with the "known", work towards what to him is the "unknown", namely, that our universe is so planned by its Creator that if we will work in harmony with

Him, all will be well; if not, we must expect trouble. "You *hurt yourself* by kicking at the goad" (Acts 26¹⁴, Moffatt). "Men punish themselves by getting into disharmony with their own constitution and that of the universe; just as a wheel in a piece of machinery punishes itself when it gets out of gear" (Charles Kingsley). On that basis, the expository preacher will proceed to show that the reference in Exodus 20⁵ to the jealousy of God is not a piece of outworn legislation emanating from a blood-thirsty tribal deity, but rather a statement of fact observed by the Jews and noted as such. And the reference in St. Luke 20¹⁷, ¹⁸ to the stone which grinds to powder is not a threat. It is a statement of sober fact, a picture of the man who seeks to live his life contrary to The Way. (I am not unmindful of the fact that in the sphere of venereal disease antibiotics now effect a speedy, painless and (apparently) lasting cure. This makes laxity in sexual morals easier, but it does not invalidate the contention that trouble ensues if divine law is flouted.)

"Look at life, Tom. Face the facts. But the Bible has been saying this all along. Oh, yes, it is very *old*. But it is not *out-dated*."

(2) What about Tom's suspicion that Christianity is narrow and confined in its origins and relevance? The Eternal is anchored in history. We cannot, and must not, avoid the "scandal of particularity", that the Word of God became flesh as a Jew in a particular town of a narrow province under Roman rule; *sub Pontio Pilato passus*. "Religion", said J. H. Newman in his *Apology*, "as a mere sentiment is to me a dream and a mockery." The roots of our faith go down deep into Jewish soil.

But we have something very definite to say in answer to his suspicion that we are concerned with his soul and that there our primary interest in him ceases. It is one of those dangerous half-truths which border on the lie. Somehow we must get it across to him that the Christian faith views him not as a soul but as a *whole*. We must bluntly face him with one of those paradoxes which go right to the heart of our faith, namely, that Christianity is at once a fundamentally *this*-worldly religion and an *other*-worldly religion. Let us look briefly at these two facets of the faith.

(*a*) Christianity is a *this*-worldly religion. It rejects *in toto* the taunt of the Communist that Christianity offers its followers "pie in the sky when they die". It is the religion of Him who said to the palsied man *both* "Thy sins be forgiven thee" *and* "Arise, take up thy bed, and go thy way into thy house" (St. Mark $2^{5, 11}$). That is to say, Jesus treated the man as an entity. To have said either of these sentences and to have left the other unsaid would have been to do violence to the essential one-ness of the body–soul relationship of the man in the story. Similar instances might be multiplied (cf. St. Mark 5^{25-34}).

(*b*) Christianity is an *other*-worldly religion. Being committed to a doctrine, not of the immortality of the soul, but of the resurrection of the body, it has much to say of the after-life, and does not blush to preach of heaven and hell, though it finds that both these terms need a very great deal of interpretation if their Biblical content is not to be radically misunderstood. It holds, with Keats, that this world is "a vale of soul-making". The fact that Christianity has this deep interest in the after-life means that it meets a man at the point of his great need. For every time he passes a cemetery or looks into the grave where he has just buried his dear one, or—if he is philosophically minded— every time he considers the nature of the universe, he is confronted by this problem. He may not realize this; or if he does, he may seek to drown the fact in an orgy of surrealistic art or of hot jazz or of business fast and furious, but he needs the strong Biblical doctrine of the world to come. It is our task to rouse him from his "worm's-eye view" of the universe and to show him life as a son of the Most High.

E

Somewhere along the line of the "marriage" of the two-sided view of Christianity as a *this*-worldly and an *other*-worldly religion will be found our answer to his suspicion that our faith is narrow and confined in its relevance.

(3) What are we to say about his suspicion that Christianity is not very concerned with social problems? I think it is a fact that, speaking generally, our generation is conscious of social wrongs and irregularities. May we not, and should we not, "cash in on" this sensitiveness? May we not do so along the lines both of history and of the exposition of the Bible?

History will provide a multitude of illustrations to show that it has been the Spirit of Christ working through members of the Body of Christ which has been the very cause of the sensitiveness of conscience which has righted social wrongs. We may mention to him, almost at random, the names of the Earl of Shaftesbury, Albert Schweitzer, F. D. Maurice, B. F. Westcott, Canon Barnett, William Temple, Trevor Huddleston and a score of others. If he has any sense of history, he will not be slow to realize that much, indeed most, of the social reform of which we are so rightly proud today had its birth within the Christian Church.

Exposition of the Bible will prove equally effective in answering Tom's suspicion. We shall point out to him that the Pentateuchal legislation, with its detailed care for women, animals, the "stranger" and so forth, all sprang from that religion where priest and doctor were one, and where God's concern for the least of His creatures was the *fons et origo* of all beneficent social activity.

We shall take him to the prophets, showing him passages whose print almost burns our fingers as we turn the pages, so strong is the writer's denunciation of international immorality, of sexual perversion, of the evils of drink, of the oppression of the poor and so on. We shall take him to the

Epistle of St. James, that most "prophetic" of the books of
the New Testament Canon. We shall turn his attention to
the teaching of our Lord on social issues such as the State,
the danger of money, the family and divorce. We shall
expound to him the Epistles of St. Paul, the profundity of
whose doctrinal teaching is paralleled only by the directness
and force of his ethical teaching.

Straight from the heart of the Bible, direct from our
expository preaching, comes the answer to Tom's suspicion.
Indeed, as we proclaim to him the central doctrine of the
Church as the Beloved Community, as the Body of Christ,
we shall show that it gives expression to the fundamental
Christian conviction that man cannot be treated just as an
individual but as a member of the social order. That social
order will be "whole" only when it is impregnated with
Christian life and insight.

(4) and (5) We may take together Tom's vague awareness
of other faiths and his innate tendency to think "scientifically" rather than "Biblically". He will only begin to see
the supremacy of Christianity over other faiths when he
begins really to understand Christianity. And he will only
begin to think Biblically as well as scientifically, Scripturally rather than secularly, when we have done for him
some serious interpretative work, translating for him the
language of Scripture into his own terminology. Let me
illustrate.

Salvation—here is a central Biblical concept. Both Old
and New Testaments are full of references to the word. But
it is true to say that no word is less understood than this
today. Say to Tom or his friends, "Are you saved?" and he
looks at you puzzled and hurt. And yet it is a matter of life
and death to get across to him the real meaning of the word.
Can we so expound the Biblical usage of the word as to
relate it to modern life? I believe we can.

We may choose three of the ways in which the word is

used within the pages of our Bible. Salvation is used: (*a*) In a *military* sense when deliverance, rescue, from a foreign enemy is under discussion (Exodus 14¹³; 15², *et passim*). *Victory*—Tom understands that; his memories of the War and our deliverance from Nazi domination are still fresh in his mind. And for all that he may aver, Tom knows something of moral defeat and the craving for rescue. (*b*) The word is used in a *naval* sense. The story of the shipwreck in Acts 27 ends with the words "they escaped all safe to land" (v. 44). The word is the one under discussion (with a prefix added). Tom, if he was in the Navy, will readily understand, as we expound to him the Pauline doctrine of salvation, how it is that the Apostle can say, "I have been saved: I am being saved: I shall be saved." Does not this triple approach to the doctrine remind him of the time when, after a shipwreck, a hand was stretched out to rescue him, and he said, "I've been saved"? Within the boat, he could say, "I'm being saved", but still there was the aspect of future salvation, a rescue not finally completed till he reached the shore. No wonder that the Church was early likened to a ship. (*c*) The word is used in a *medical* sense. In the same passage in the Acts when St. Paul bids the sailors take food, he says, "This is for your health (salvation)" (27³⁴). We may note also Philippians 1¹⁹, "this shall turn out for my welfare", and 2¹², "work out your full spiritual health"; St. Mark 5³⁴ and St. Luke 7⁵⁰ are also relevant. The word is similarly used in the papyri, and indeed in our liturgy ("grant us Thy salvation").

Let us take another illustration of a Biblical concept where in our expository preaching a good deal of "translation" work will be necessary. *Peace*—here is one of the big words of the Bible. It is used, of course, just as we used it when, the War over, a great sigh of relief went up all over the world; peace had come. It is the cessation of hostilities. Tom knows all about that. And from that "known" we may proceed to the "unknown", namely, the fact that man by his wilfulness is in a state of hostility Godwards, nor will he know peace till George Matheson's prayer has been answered in his case:

> Force me to render up my sword
> And I shall conqueror be.

That is the military sense of the word. But there is another usage which, for want of a better adjective, we may describe as the psychological. What do we mean when we quote St. Paul: "The fruit of the Spirit is . . . peace"? Or when we say, "The peace of God, which passeth all understanding . . ."?

Let us start again with the "known". There was a man who in the twenties or thirties of this century had ruined his body and mind in the mad rush to "get rich quick". In his despair he went to a psychiatrist, who asked him what place religion occupied in his life. He was so surprised at the question that he could not find an answer. The psychiatrist went on: "There is one kind of patient I hardly ever find in my consulting-room. It is the man at the heart of whose life is Christianity." From the "known" we pass to the "unknown". We point Tom, for example, to the stories in the Gospels of two women in need who came to our Lord, one the woman with the haemorrhage, the other the "woman who was a sinner". To both, the message of Jesus was "Go in peace" (St. Mark 5[34]; St. Luke 7[50]). He integrated those two broken personalities; He made them whole. They passed from disharmony into peace, because of their contact with Him, the Lord of Life. We shall, on the basis of life around and of the Bible which we are expounding, point out to Tom that his generation and ours is faced with the alternative of "going to pieces" (of which there are many signs) or of "going to peace", that is, to life lived according to the mind and in the power of Christ.

Faith; Redemption; Blood; and a dozen other familiar terms—how much they mean to us! How little to those to whom we are sent! But Tom and his friends will never know life at its fullest and best until they enter into the meaning of such concepts as these, until the language of Zion becomes real to them. But before that takes place, we expository preachers have translation work to do as radical in its nature as that which faced John Wycliffe in translating from the Latin into the vulgar tongue. Only too often, through our culpable laziness in failing to enter into Tom's outlook, we sin after the fashion of the Cambridge don of whom E. L. Mascall tells in one of his books. He began his sermon to a group of Cambridge bedmakers, so the story runs, with the following words: "The ontological argument for the existence of God has in recent years, largely under Teutonic influence, been relegated to a position of comparative inferiority in the armoury of Christian apologetics."

No: it will not do. We must see life through Tom's eyes; breathe his atmosphere; sit where he sits. Then we must get busy with the work of translation. Our equipment? A prayer desk; all the apparatus that scholarship will provide; a red pencil of large proportion as again and again we work through the drafts of our expository preaching. Our reward? The light in Tom's eyes as it dawns on him that there is an authoritative Word of God for him and his generation; that Christianity is concerned with him as a man in all the complexity of his manhood, concerned with him here and now, concerned with him hereafter, concerned with him as an individual and in the wider sphere of his social contacts; that the Christian faith is the most relevant and up-to-date thing in the world; that "God has spoken . . . to us . . . in His Son".

VI

THE PREACHER AS MAN OF GOD

St. Alphonsus de Liguori tells of a bishop who, preaching to a congregation which included St. Francis de Sales, gave a very ornate and learned discourse. Much applause followed. St. Francis remained silent. The bishop asked him how he liked the sermon. "You pleased all but One," was the saint's reply.

More than once, in the preceding chapters, it has been indicated that real preaching implies certain qualifications in the man who undertakes the task. For instance, when we were trying to feel our way towards a definition of preaching (p. 24), we saw the inadequacy of Phillips Brooks' definition, "The communication of truth by man to men", if only because it does not indicate what kind of man may preach. We asked: "Can *anyone* preach?" The answer was clearly "No". There is a difference between an essay and a sermon, between a thesis and a sermon, and the difference is not wholly in the subject-matter. Have we not all had the experience, at some time, of listening to a man preach whose technical qualifications were obviously deficient? We could have wished for a more adequate academic background, perhaps even for more correct grammar. Had we wanted to do so, we might have quarrelled with his Biblical exegesis, or with his analysis of the contemporary situation. But, as we have pondered on what he said, we have realized that his utterance could rightly be called a *sermon*. Here was a man of God, standing between Divine grace and human need and, by means of the spoken word, linking the two. The experience may not have been an entirely welcome one to us. It was a searching and a humbling one. It reminded

us of the Pauline word: "Though I speak with the tongues
of men and of angels . . . though I . . . understand all
mysteries and all knowledge . . . and have not love, I am
nothing" (1 Corinthians 13[1, 2]).

"Here was a man of God," we said as we listened. The
verb was significant. We did not say he *possessed* (or did not
possess) a degree; or that he had *achieved* (or failed to
achieve) a mastery of English, though both these things in
themselves were highly desirable. We pushed our way
past the outward accoutrements to the man himself.
"Here *was* a man of God." The cynic was right who said,
"What you *are* speaks so loud that I cannot hear what
you say", and that is nowhere truer than in the realm of
preaching. What the preacher *is* is more important than
what he *has*.

It comes to this, that the preacher must never cease to
bear in mind, and to work out in experience, the meaning
of the fundamental Christian paradox "I . . . . yet not I"
(Galatians 2[20]). One who heard Dr. Alexander Whyte
preach said that he saw in him the perfect tension of that
paradox, a tension which gave the power to his preaching.
"I"—no one but Alexander Whyte could have preached
that sermon. "Not I"—Alexander Whyte was sufficiently
unobtrusive for his Lord to be seen.

This is a matter of no small importance. Personality is a
God-given thing, to be accepted and rejoiced in. David
cannot wear Saul's armour—nor should he try to. We may
learn from others; there is a freemasonry of preaching as
there is a freemasonry of scholarship. But to be a feeble
imitation of the great is to degrade one's own God-given
personality. It is said that when Dr. Winnington-Ingram
was at the height of his power and popularity as Bishop of
London and exercising a great influence over young men,
there were multitudes of young clergy who copied his style
and mannerisms; some even went so far as to read his

sermons as if they were their own. (One such young man learned his lesson when he began doing this one Sunday in his pulpit, without having taken the precaution of looking over the sermon first. The young clergyman began: "When I was Bishop of Stepney . . ."!) The preacher must learn to give his personality unreservedly to the God who gave it to him and then to receive it back enhanced and enriched. He must learn to magnify his *office* (Romans 11¹³), but never to magnify *himself*, lest in so doing he obscure men's vision of the Christ whom he preaches. He must learn the meaning of that Biblical humility which consists not of an under-estimate of oneself and one's gifts (after the manner of Uriah Heap), but of a *true* estimate of oneself and of a realization of the fact that one's gifts are precisely that—*gifts* given by God for the edifying of the Body of Christ. This will lead to yet another paradox which will give power to the preacher's work, the paradox of trembling and of confidence.

"Do you work in fear and trembling?" said Blake to Samuel Palmer, who had come to sit at his feet. "Indeed I do, sir." "Then you'll do," answered the master. That attitude of trembling, induced by the magnitude of the task on which he is engaged, will cast the preacher back on the Master who commissioned him and who, by His Spirit, empowers him. That in turn will breed a quiet God-centred confidence.

From one point of view, the Bible is a collection of biographies, some fragmentary, some more detailed, of men who, in their day and to the men of their generation and of succeeding generations, were agents of the revelation of God. In the context of this book we might say that the Bible is a collection of preachers' biographies. This is most obvious within the compass of the Old Testament in the case of the prophets. Of them we have already said a little (*vide supra*, pp. 40ff.), in connection with the sense of trusteeship which weighed on them like a burden heavy to be borne. But there is much more to it than this. Does not the writer of 2 Peter (2⁵) speak of Noah as "a preacher of righteousness", suggesting in this phrase that God sought, even in the dim ages before the flood, to use this means of self-communication to men?

A study of the great figures of the Old Testament is, from this point of view, a study of God's preachers, for an Abraham in his day, and a Moses at a later epoch, each became the means of God's self-disclosure to men in their need. This, indeed, is a fruitful line of study for those of us who, in however small a way, find ourselves in their succession. Let me illustrate from the two names which I have mentioned.

The Biblical material for the study of Abraham is abundant. Not only are there the stories of Genesis (Chapters 17ff.), but also the great passages in the Pauline letters in which Abraham is the central figure (especially Romans 4 and Galatians 3 and 4). And special note should be taken of Hebrews 11⁸⁻¹⁰. The views of scholars on Abraham differ widely, and will continue to do so. But few would debate the point that, with his advent, a new chapter opened in the story of religion and of man's relation to the Infinite. Sir Leonard Woolley has put us in his debt by helping us to understand the world of Abraham's day, the magnificence of Ur with its splendid architecture, its lovely lapis lazuli work and its very considerable culture. Indeed, one of the best commentaries on the life of Abraham is a study of Woolley's sumptuously illustrated volumes, *Ur Excavations*, especially Volume II, *The Royal Cemetery* (Text and Plates, 1934, published for the Trustees of the British Museum and of the Museum of the University of Pennsylvania Expedition to Mesopotamia). Those who are denied access to these books may get the feel of Ur and its civilization by reading Woolley's *Abraham: Recent Discoveries and Hebrew Origins*

(Faber & Faber, 1936). Against that background, we ask ourselves: What was it which made Abraham obey, "when he was called to go out into a place which he should after receive for an inheritance", going out "not knowing whither he went" (Hebrews 11[8])? And by means of this ancient figure, looming up, as it were, out of the mists of antiquity, we are compelled to face the meaning of faith, that utterly daring reliance on an unseen God, the architect and maker of a city whose foundations were surer even than those of Ur.

There is an insight into the character of Abraham, which is of importance to the preacher, given to us in Romans 4[19]. It comes to us, strangely enough, in connection with a textual variant reading. The Apostle is writing of the incident of the birth to Abraham and Sara in their old age of a son (Genesis 17 and 21). Certain manuscripts and versions have a negative before the verb "considered"; some have not. Strange as it may seem, both readings make sense, and both shed a light on the character of Abraham in this hour of crisis in his development. Those manuscripts and versions which have the negative (Cod. Bezae, Sangermanensis, Augiensis, etc.; Old Latin, Harclean Syriac, etc.) give us the picture of a man "reckoning as of no importance" the (otherwise) appalling facts of old age come to himself and to Sara, and with old age no son. He could thus reckon these facts of no importance in as much as he offset against them the faithfulness of the God who had promised. Those manuscripts and versions which do *not* give the negative (Cod. Sinaiticus, Alexandrinus, Vaticanus, Ephraemi, etc.; Vulgate, Peshitta, etc.) give us the picture of a man who "gave the facts their full weight and faced them" and yet "staggered not at the promise of God through unbelief". It is not often, in matters of textual criticism, that the presence or absence of a negative leads essentially to the same sense, while giving a slightly different slant on the character of the person who is the subject of the verb. But so it is in this case; and there stands out in bold relief the magnificent figure of a man of God, a man of faith, who, precisely because he was *that*, could be the medium of God's revelation to men. With a sure insight, the writer of the Epistle to the Hebrews reiterated "By faith . . . by faith" ($11^{8, 9}$).

We turn to the figure of Moses. Again the Biblical material is abundant. Not only are there the stories of Exodus (*passim*), but also passages in the Acts of the Apostles and the Epistle to the Hebrews which throw a light on an epoch-making figure (especially Acts 7 and Hebrews 11^{23-28}). The verses in the eleventh chapter of the Epistle to the Hebrews are particularly suggestive. Someone has wisely said that the life of Moses, as recorded in the book of Exodus, can be divided up into three periods of forty years each. In the first period, spent in the luxury of the Egyptian court, he learned how great he was. In the second period, spent in the obscurity of tending his father-in-law's flock, he learned how small he was. In the third and last period, spent in leading a rebellious rabble through a wild and unknown desert to the borders of the Promised Land, he learned how great God was. It may be affirmed that most men who, in any sense, become the media of God's self-disclosure, have to learn that lesson, and they generally do so in that order, their early pride and self-sufficiency being broken and giving way to a realization of the greatness and adequacy of God.

So experience would seem to suggest. And so the commentary of Hebrews 11^{23-28} would seem to affirm. The long series of verbs in these verses is profoundly suggestive. "He *refused* to be called the son of Pharaoh's daughter; he *chose* to suffer . . . he *esteemed* reproach for Christ . . . he *forsook* Egypt . . . he *endured* . . ." Strong verbs these; verbs which speak of renunciation, of a severe simplicity, of

an element of austerity, even of "asceticism", if we bear
in mind that that last word is a transliteration of a Greek
word which means training. Richard Church was thinking
of the value of renunciation when, in the second volume
of his autobiography, he refers to it as "the wisdom of
travelling light".

If the story of Abraham indicates that the man God uses
is a man of faith, the story of Moses indicates that there
must be in him an element of self-discipline and of renunciation. This is corroborated by experience and by Scripture.
The preacher is a specialist, but no specialist ever achieves
his goal without a very big element of sacrifice in his life.
The great pianist, Paderewski, used to say: "If I miss my
practice one day, I know it; if I miss it two days, the
experts know; if I miss it three days, my audience knows
it." Readers of the life of Yehudi Menuhin by Robert
Magidoff (Robert Hale, Ltd., 1956) will recall how stern
was the discipline of the early years and later that dark
period when it seemed that, at a comparatively advanced
age, the great violinist had to learn his art almost all over
again (Chapters 7 and 15 are particularly instructive).

It we may hazard a guess, we would say that the preaching
effectiveness of far more men has been lost through inattention to this basic matter of self-control, of discipline,
even of renunciation, than through what are normally
regarded as the "big sins". Many a man who knows well
the Christian doctrine of the human body nevertheless
abuses the body with which he has been entrusted. He
realizes that, in the words of William Temple, Christianity
is the most materialistic of all religions; that it is a heresy to
hold, as did the Gnostics, that matter is evil. On the
contrary, he knows that it is the basic teaching of the
Christian faith that one's body is the temple of the Holy
Ghost (1 Corinthians 3^{16}, 2 Corinthians 6^{16}—it is con-
ceivable that this saying goes back to an unrecorded *logion*

of Jesus which lies behind such a reference as St. John 2²¹);
that we are not our own, we have been bought with a price
(1 Corinthians 6¹⁹, ²⁰); that, so far from regarding the body
as a mere "tomb" of the spirit (cf. Plato's play on words—
τὸ μὲν σῶμα ἐστιν ἡμῖν σῆμα, Gorg. 493A), a religion
which is based on doctrines of Incarnation and the resurrection of the body can scarcely exaggerate the importance of
the physical in the spiritual life. And yet, knowing all this
and accepting it as part of his theological outlook, how often
does the man of God allow his ministry to be vitiated by
inattention to the demands of his body.

That inattention may take various forms. It is a form of
lack of self-control, in many cases, to become so obsessed
with one's work as to be unfit to fulfil it. "The sins of good
people come chiefly from exhaustion." The warning is
from Father Paul Bull (*Lectures on Preaching and Sermon
Construction* (S.P.C.K., 1932), p. 95), and it finds corrobora-
tion in the lives of multitudes of men who, tense and over-
wrought themselves, are unable to minister to others in
similar need. On this point, there is instruction in the
story of Elijah recorded in 1 Kings 18 and 19. The shattering experience on Carmel lay behind the prophet. Then,
naturally enough, reaction set in, with the feeling known to
most sensitive men, of exhaustion and depression (19⁴).
What was needed to set him on his feet again? Many of us
would have suggested a retreat or a convention or at least a
summer school. The divine provision was something far
less "spiritual". It was sleep and food (v. 5)! Let each
man find out, by experiment, the minimum sleep which
he needs for maximum efficiency in his work, and then
let him so discipline himself as to regulate his time-table
accordingly. So will sloth be avoided on the one hand;
and, on the other, that hectic approach to life which impairs
his own efficiency and renders him useless in his ministry
to others.

If too little sleep is the besetting sin of some men of God, too much sleep is the besetting sin of others. Most of us find that, if we have not had our period of quiet with God fairly early in the morning it is unlikely that we shall get it undisturbed later on. The post comes in; the telephone begins to ring; there are appointments to keep and callers to see. It is a case of early in the morning, or not at all. The early rising thus called for demands discipline in going to bed the night before and curtailing, sometimes, the social hour which we naturally enjoy. It is the price we pay for spiritual efficiency. Jeremiah tells us that "God rises up early" to send His prophets. John Oman commented on this: "Naturally His prophets should follow His example!" The words of Calvin condemn most of us in this connection: "Oh what deep-seated malice against God is this, that I will do anything and everything but to go to Him and remain with Him in secret prayer!" The cases of barristers are won in their chambers: the battles of a man's character, of his preaching and of his general ministry are won on his knees in his room or in his church.

Indiscipline attacks others in even more subtle ways. Gradually, almost unnoticed, a habit grows on a man; almost before he realizes it, it is beginning to dominate him. In time of stress his hand habitually goes to the pocket where his cigarette-case lies, whereas an upward glance to his Lord would be at once more effective and more fitting. "All things are lawful for me"—certainly no man must dare to legislate for another in any matter of personal habit. "But I will not be brought under the power of any" (1 Corinthians 6[12])—that is a salutary warning to which we all should do well to give heed. The body is a magnificent slave; it can be a tyrannical master. If "the fruit of the Spirit is love", it is also "self-control" (Galatians 5[22, 23]).

St. Augustine, in this as in so many matters, put it suc-
cinctly and pointedly:

> To my fellow men a heart of love,
> To my God a heart of flame,
> To myself a heart of steel;

or again:

> Cujus vita fulgur
> Ejus verba tonitur—

"he whose life is lightning-bright, *his* words are like a
thunder-clap".

The Pastoral Epistles provide a rewarding study for any
would-be man of God. That much-to-be-coveted title
occurs in the context both of *fight* and of *flight* (1 Timothy
6[11, 12]). If there is to be a "good fight of faith" (v. 12),
there must necessarily be "flight" (v. 11) from those things
which make the man of God soft. He will, of course, "flee
fornication" (1 Corinthians 6[18]); he will, of course, "flee
from idolatry" (1 Corinthians 10[14]). He will need to be
more on the alert against those subtler sins which slip in
almost unheeded and which sap the sources of his spiritual
energy. If that happens, he will find himself like the false
prophet in *The Shepherd of Hermas* (*The Shepherd of Hermas*,
Mandate 11), who, "empty himself, giveth empty answers
to empty enquirers". Jeremiah had a sharp word to say of
those who were themselves so barren of a message from
God that they were compelled to "steal" the Lord's words
"every man from his neighbour"; "they use their *tongues*
and say 'He saith' " (Jeremiah 23[30, 31]). It takes a good
deal more than a man's tongue to say that, with any self-
authenticating conviction. It takes all there is of a man of
God. "Some men prepare their sermons; other men prepare themselves." The truth is, of course, that both
preparations are called for and are entirely necessary, and

there is no resting from either so long as the preaching ministry lasts.

Looking back over the ground we have so far covered in this chapter, we have begun to view the Bible as a collection of biographies of preachers. A glance at the towering figure of Abraham has shown us the essential ingredient of faith in the make-up of the man of God; Moses has taught us lessons in self-control and discipline. The scope of such Biblical study is almost limitless. Elsewhere I have sought to show how this study can be pursued if we work on the Biblical material connected with the character of our Lord, of John the Baptist and of St. Paul (*The Ministry of the Word* (The Canterbury Press, 1945), Chapters 2–4). I will not repeat it here, though it is a fruitful and a challenging course of study. Rather, I will close this chapter with a brief study of one chapter of one of the Pauline epistles, as being in itself a revelation of the type of man whom God uses in His Self-disclosure.

There are few passages in all the Pauline corpus which show us the writer himself more clearly than does the second chapter of the first Epistle to the Thessalonians. It was not the intention of the writer to provide us with an outline of many of the requirements in the life and character of a preacher. But that is precisely what he does, and for that provision we may be thankful. Among such characteristics we note:

(i) *Boldness* (v. 2). The abominable treatment which the Apostle had received at Philippi did not serve to intimidate him. (The reference is, of course, to Acts 16 and the beatings and imprisonment accorded to St. Paul and Silas there.) When he came to Thessalonica he found himself possessed of a God-given courage which could calmly face opposition.

(ii) *A sense of stewardship* (vv. 4–6). We note again that

F

tone of awed surprise at being "put in trust with the Gospel" on which we remarked earlier (*supra*, p. 43). His stewardship is never taken for granted. His aim is to please the God who "knows him through and through" (Phillips), and this saves him from the preacher's perennial temptation of preaching to the gallery.

(iii) *Gentleness* (v. 7). Judging by the gesticulations of some men in the pulpit, one would imagine that it was possible to drive men into the Kingdom. Their threatening finger and menacing attitude give substance to the gibe that the pulpit is the coward's castle, for there can be no retaliation on the part of the long-suffering occupants of the pew. Not so did St. Paul do his work. He knew that far more is done in the cause of Christ by the gentle touch—he compares himself to a nurse!—than by the shout and the threat. Had not Ananias put his hands on Saul the persecutor and called him "brother"? And had not that done more for him than any amount of heated argumentation?

(iv) *Self-giving* (v. 8). "It was a joy to us to give you not only the Gospel of God but our very hearts—so dear did you become to us" (Phillips). It may be doubted whether any preaching is of much avail which does not involve just that; which, as the saying goes, does not "take it out of you". For if the man in the pew is to be a recipient, the man in the pulpit must be a giver, a giver of his very heart. Preaching is for the healing of men sick with sin. As in the case of the Master, of whom it is recorded that in His healing activity "virtue went out of Him" (cf. St. Mark 5^{30}, St. Luke 6^{19}, 8^{46}), so in the case of the disciple. Men made a rough guess at the age of Jesus, and they put Him round about fifty (St. John 8^{57}). But He was only thirty! Is there something to be said for the suggestion that those years in the Ministry had aged Him? Be that as it may, the preaching which does not "take it out of you" has little to give to others.

(v) *Honest hard work* (vv. 9–10). This is not the only

passage in the Pauline letters in which the Apostle stresses the importance he attached to independence gained by doing a secular job (Acts 20^{34}, cf. 1 Corinthians 9$^{11,\ 12}$; 2 Corinthians 11^9). If the majority of us who preach today "live of the Gospel" and not by "secular" means, at least it should be evident for all to see that we work quite as hard as, if not much harder than, those who catch the eight-ten train to business every morning. There are few sins in the clergy which the laity find it harder to forgive than laziness. Their instinct in this regard is dead right. How can they respect a man who lies abed when they are on their way to work? The old description of a clergyman as being "on six days invisible and on the seventh incomprehensible" does little to adorn or to commend the Gospel.

(vi) *Stimulating strength* (v. 11). The gentleness of the nurse of verse 7 gives place here to the strength of the father, stimulating, encouraging, instructing. Men's hearts fail them for fear. They need the strengthening stimulus which comes from a man who, in the Scottish phrase, is "far ben wi' God", who himself has learned to lean hard on the eternal changelessness of God and so can "stretch out a loving hand to wrestlers with the troubled sea".

(vii) *Deep affection* (vv. 17–20). These Thessalonian Christians were the pride and joy of St. Paul's heart. He had for them an affection so deep and sincere as to make separation from them a matter of pain. They were not perfect; indeed, there is evidence in this correspondence that they got the Apostle's teaching wrong and gravely misunderstood him. But a parent loves a child in spite of its foolishness and naughtiness. So with the man of God and the children of God entrusted to him. There are bonds of affection which bind them very close together. One is forced to ask some searching questions when one meets the vicar whose successive parishes are *always* the most difficult in the country and whose people are quite impossible.

"The fault, dear Brutus . . ."? Has the Vicar concerned got that overwhelming love for his flock which enables him to see how much good there is in them, and, seeing and appreciating it, to nourish and stimulate it?

George Herbert, whose book *The Country Parson* has deservedly become one of the classics of our religious literature and whose almost hidden ministry has become an example on which many others have sought to model their own, entitles his seventh chapter "The Parson Preaching". It is full of practical suggestions—George Herbert knows how to make a point. He refers to the sayings and stories which country folk will remember. "By these and other means the Parson procures attention; but the character"— he uses the word in the sense of characteristic or essential peculiarity—"of his Sermon is Holiness; he is not witty, or learned, or eloquent, but Holy." There is no more to be said than that.

VII

PREACHING AS CORPORATE WORSHIP

WHETHER it is apocryphal or not I am not sure, but the story has gained currency that a Chicago newspaper reported on a Free Church Service as follows: "The Reverend A. B. then gave the finest prayer ever offered to a Chicago audience." True or untrue, the present writer heard an incumbent apologize for the absence of members of his choir owing to an epidemic of influenza with consequent alterations in the plans for music at Evensong. "I am sorry", he said, "that we are unable this evening to give you (*sic!*) the rendering of the *Magnificat* and *Nunc Dimittis* which we had intended!"

A slip of the tongue? Maybe. Or was it indicative of our all too frequent forgetfulness of the fact that every act of worship is an offering to Almighty God?

> In Thy house, great God, we offer
>   Of Thine own to Thee;
> And for Thine acceptance proffer,
>   All unworthily,
> Hearts and minds and hands and voices,
>   In our choicest
> Psalmody.

The liturgy and music, offered to God with maximum care and loving attention to detail, are themselves a sacramental act. Such an act points to the fact that for the Christian man, *all* life is worship. Zechariah looked forward to the day when the bells of the horses would have marked upon them "Holiness unto the Lord", and the pots in the Lord's house would be like the bowls before the altar (Zechariah

14[20, 21]). That is to say, there would be no divide between
sacred and secular; everything done would be an offering
to the Most High. For the Christian the day to which the
prophet looked forward has arrived, ushered in by the
Incarnation of the Word. Whatever he does, be it washing
up or serving in a shop, be it reading faithfully pursued or
visiting dutifully performed, all is "Holiness unto the
Lord"; all are acts of divine worship.

For the preacher, his craft ranks high in those acts of
worship which he offers to the Lord. In those twenty
minutes on Sunday morning or evening he offers up to God
the best that he has. Into those minutes are compressed the
fruits of the preparation of the preceding week and of his
exegetical wrestlings. More than that, he has been toiling
with the stuff of men's problems in the light of God's
revelation in Christ mediated by the Holy Spirit; and he
has been seeking to find the most suitable medium of
expression for eternal truth to men who are totally unaccustomed to Hebraic thought-forms. The results of all
this he now offers to God in the sermon, which now is seen
to be an act of worship worthy of a thinking man (cf.
Romans 12[1], $\tau\dot{\eta}\nu$ $\lambda o\gamma\iota\kappa\dot{\eta}\nu$ $\lambda\alpha\tau\rho\epsilon\dot{\iota}\alpha\nu$ $\dot{\upsilon}\mu\hat{\omega}\nu$—"a service to
God such as befits the reason", Sanday and Headlam *in loc*.).
Here is an art, the highest art known to man, dedicated to
Him who has entrusted it to him. Here is an offering of
mind and thought, of speech, of diction and of presentation,
made to the Creator-God who gave these faculties for
human use. Only when preaching is envisaged thus can the
invocation "In the Name of the Father, and of the Son, and
of the Holy Ghost" have full meaning; as things are today,
familiarity with this invocation has bred contempt, and it is
too lightly used and too rapidly gabbled. "Worship is
man's acknowledgement of the worth-ship of God with
every part of his being" (Bishop Colin Dunlop, *Anglican
Public Worship*, p. 19). Preaching provides the preacher

with a magnificent opportunity to give expression to this.
To do it, he must know the meaning of what Amy Wilson
Carmichael once wrote in one of her poems:

> So would I tread where Thou hast trod,
> My spirit *tender of the glory of God*.

All this is the natural outcome of what has been said in
previous chapters. But here I am concerned to go further.
For preaching is not only an act of worship on the part of
the preacher. It is an act of *corporate* worship, an action of
the Body of Christ. On this important facet of preaching,
on preaching as corporate worship, singularly little appears
to have been written, when we consider the quantity of
writing which has been produced in the field of homiletics.
To the consideration of this aspect of preaching we now
turn.

Mr. Gladstone in his *Homeric Studies* wrote: "The work
of the orator from its very inception is inextricably mixed
up with practice. It is cast in the mould offered to him by
the minds of his hearers. It is an influence principally received from his audience (so to speak) in vapour, which he
pours back on them in a flood. The sympathy and con-
currence of his time is, with his own mind, joint parent of
the work." It is deeply interesting that one who had trained
himself meticulously in the art of public speaking, and had
studied and absorbed Quintilian and Cicero, could yet
write: "I wish you knew the state of total impotence to
which I should be reduced if there were no echo to the
accents of my own voice." In similar vein, Dame Sybil
Thorndike, broadcasting on June 22nd, 1954, said in
reference to the effect of the audience on an actor or actress:
"The quality of the audience makes all the difference in the
world."

So much for secular illustrations. To come nearer home
—any preacher of experience will bear witness to this fact,

that in Church A one Sunday, having prepared himself and his sermon with care and prayer, he finds that his words rebound like a fives ball from the wall of the court. In Church B the following Sunday, the preparation of himself and of his sermon having been the same as during the previous week, he finds a receptivity to the Word of God and a response to it so manifest and real as to be almost tangible. What is the reason for this? No doubt many factors are involved. I suspect, however, that one of the most important is this—the members of congregation A have never grasped the fact that preaching is a function, a corporate activity, of the Church. They come to listen, perchance to indulge in "a little folding of the hands in sleep", perhaps to find fuel for an interesting criticism over lunch of the parson's jejune effort. But at Church B the members of the congregation know that prayerful dedication on the part of the preacher is not enough—something is demanded of *them*. Preaching is a *corporate* activity. It is not likely that all the members of congregation B have learned that lesson, but a "godly remnant" has. And God has a way of working His strange work through godly remnants at various stages in the world's history; and he still does it, even at St. Agatha's in 1958.

A friend of the writer's found his preaching work something of a grim battle. Then there came a time when, to use his own words, he had "come out of the tunnel". He did not expect that preaching thenceforward would be easy, but he knew that he was out into the light and that preaching would be a different thing from that time on. When asked if he could put his finger on the reason for this, he said he had shared his difficulties with about three members of his parish. They had promised to pray. In this way his preaching was more than an individual effort; it had become the work of the Body of Christ in that parish.

Here our doctrine of the Body of Christ links up with our

doctrine of the Holy Spirit, Who is indeed the *Spirit of the Body*. Canon C. E. Raven, in the Gifford Lectures for 1951–52, wrote of the fellowship:

"As the several members find each its proper function in the economy of the whole, their fellowship develops a spontaneous co-operation in obedience to the creative guidance of the indwelling Spirit; each individual unit finds his freedom in the voluntary service of the whole, the whole is possessed of the full power and resources of its constituents. To describe it as 'one body and one Spirit' is no exaggeration; and available for it are the resources of God. Sensitiveness integrates the community as the barriers of individuality are transcended; creativity inspires it as it gains release from fears and selfish ambitions; power without limit is at its disposal when there is no longer the wastage of inward conflict and when the Spirit of Christ is given free course" (*Natural Religion and Christian Theology. Second Series: Experience and Interpretation* (Cambridge University Press, 1953), p. 176).

Examine preaching as an act of worship a little more closely, and we find:

(i) It is an offering of *prayer*. "If two of you shall agree on earth as touching anything that they shall ask, it shall be done for them of My Father" (St. Matthew 18[19]). The prayers of the faithful have upheld the preacher during the week and in moments of quiet preparation before the service. Even during the sermon a shaft of ejaculatory prayer sometimes rises to God from a member of the congregation. More than this, the whole atmosphere in which the preaching takes place is an atmosphere of prayer.

(ii) It is an offering of the *mind*. "Thou shalt love the Lord thy God with all thy . . . mind." That is the divine command. Here is a group of men and women dedicated to

this task. They have in view the grasping of some truth
which hitherto they have not seen or which they have
neglected or misunderstood or got out of proportion in the
great revelation of God. They come to Church with their
minds "erect to Almighty God" (the phrase is quoted by
Bishop Colin Dunlop, *op. cit.*, p. 64, from the preface
attached to the English Litany on its first appearance in
1544).

(iii) It is an offering of the *will*, for the carrying into
practice of what has been learned of the mind of God
through the preaching. Preaching can never be simply
mental gymnastics, either for preacher or for congregation.
At some point it must assault the *will*. And worship takes
place when a man utters his Amen, his assent to the divine
assault, when he offers himself in response to the divine
coming in the word preached.

Much patience and perseverance will be called for in
getting our people to understand the truth of which we have
been writing above, that preaching is corporate worship.
Long years of regarding the sermon as something done by
the speaker have left deep marks on the minds of our
people. We shall not eradicate these marks overnight.
Patiently, prayerfully, persistently, we shall teach that when
the vicar or curate enters the pulpit *the Church goes into
action* in a great act of corporate worship, in prayer, in
offering of the mind, in offering of the will. This we shall
teach, and a remnant will glimpse it. In that remnant (a
remnant which, please God, will steadily grow) lies our
hope.

A further point must be made in this connection. We
shall need to think out, and slowly work out, the bearing
of this truth on the conduct of our Services. Many churches
in recent years have proved that a 9.30 or 10 a.m. celebra-
tion of the Holy Communion meets the need of people

better than services held at the more usual hours of 8 and
11 a.m. There is much to be said for this and for the break-
fast which often follows it—a practical and very real bit of
parish fellowship. But there are dangers. If what we have
said about preaching is true, five-to-ten-minute sermons
squeezed into the Holy Communion Service *will not do*.
In addition, those five or ten minutes tend in the context
of the Holy Communion to be occupied almost exclusively
with the theme of Holy Communion itself. This, it need
not be said, is a subject of immense importance. But the
task of preaching is wider than this, inasmuch as the
preacher must seek to cover "the *whole* counsel of God".
We would not be so foolish as to try to play off, the one
against the other, the ministry of Word and Sacrament.
That would indeed be foolish, and as un-Biblical as it is un-
Anglican. Both are ministries of the Grace of God. Both
are *verba Dei*. But we must seek to keep a right proportion.
We must resist to the death the attitude which says, "The
sermon matters comparatively little—it is the *worship* that
matters." That we have seen to be a contradiction in
terms. "People come to worship, not to listen to sermons"—with that we will have nothing to do. Again, we
shall resist to the death the attitude which looks on everything up to the notices as what in some circles are called
"the preliminary exercises", to be followed, as soon as
decently may be, by the "real thing"—the sermon. *Both*
are corporate worship.

Rather, in the context of Matins or Evensong, we shall
say at the end of the Third Collect or of the prayers succeeding it, "That is the end of Part I of our corporate
worship. Now together we move forward to its worthy
climax, the next act of corporate worship—the sermon".
In the context of the Holy Communion we shall say,
"Behold what manner of love the Father hath bestowed
upon us—*look*! The Body broken, the Blood outpoured.

Listen! The Word preached. 'Holy, Holy, Holy, Lord God of Hosts, heaven and earth are full of Thy glory: Glory be to Thee, O Lord, Most High.' "

We have noticed the strange lack in the text-books of this emphasis on preaching as corporate worship. An exception, in this as in so many important matters of theology, is to be found in the writings of P. T. Forsyth. In his great book *Positive Preaching and the Modern Mind* (The Lyman Beecher Lecture on Preaching, Yale University, 1907; Hodder & Stoughton, 1907), he has a chapter entitled "The Preacher and his Church, or Preaching as Worship". One cannot refuse the temptation to quote a few sentences almost at random. Having described preaching as "a sacramental act, done together with the community in the name and the power of Christ's redeeming Act and our common faith", Forsyth asks: "Are our sermons action sermons? If they are not . . . is it because they lack behind them the volume of a Church's conviction, a Church's faith, the impact of a whole Church's rule?" "The word is living only in a living community." "Preaching is the organised Hallelujah of an ordered community." "Preaching . . . is the Church confessing its faith." So we could go on quoting from a memorable chapter. But it is unnecessary. For, once we envisage preaching as "the organised Hallelujah of an ordered community", there need be little fear that we shall feel, as did Mr. Gerald Bullet's Nicky, after going to Evensong in a country parish church, that "God, if he ever attended the place of worship, always slipped quietly out, it seemed, just before the sermon".

"A sacramental act." If one thing has become clear about early Eucharistic worship it is this—*it was the corporate act of the whole Church*. As a priestly society, the Church acted corporately whenever the Eucharist was celebrated. In the words of Dom Gregory Dix (*The Shape of the Liturgy*, pp. 29–30): "*The whole Church* prayed in the

person of Christ; the *whole Church* was charged with the
office of proclaiming the revelation of Christ; the *whole
Church* offered the Eucharist as the re-calling before God
and man of the offering of Christ. . . . Christ and His
Church are one, with one mission, one life, one prayer, one
Gospel, one offering, one being, one Father."

Would to God that we could see this with equal clarity
in relation to the "sacrament of the Word"! "The sermon
is neither a moral diatribe nor an exhibition of the
preacher's views upon religion, but a setting forth of Christ
crucified and risen; it is in very truth an Elevation of the
Host" (quoted in G. Rogers, *A Rebel at Heart*, p. 279, as
from Robert Micklem). If this is true, the congregation is
"in on" this just as they are "in on" the central act of the
Eucharist. The act of preaching is not something done by
the man up in the pulpit, any more than the Holy Communion is an act done by the man who stands far away at
the Lord's Table. Both are acts of the Body corporate,
every member in his own office having his own function to
perform. "It would seem", wrote Father S. M. Gibbard
in a most interesting essay (*The Christian Mystery* in *Studies
in Ephesians*, edited by F. L. Cross (A. R. Mowbray & Co.,
1956), p. 117), "that in the early Church it was as incumbent upon the president at the Eucharistic assembly to
preach the word as to break the bread. Would that it were
so again!" If the argument outlined above is true, we can
understand the reason. The sacrament of the Word and
the sacrament of the Body and Blood of Christ went along-
side of one another, and both were corporate acts of the
Church of Christ. Perhaps the Spirit of God will grant His
Church to see this again. Only then shall we view preaching
as the holy thing which it is.

VIII

TO READ OR NOT TO READ?

SHOULD the sermon be read or not?—that is the question to which practically every young preacher has to address himself, and which many an older man in the full flush of his ministry does wisely to review from time to time. If the answer to that question were merely a matter of technique, this would scarcely be the book in which to seek to deal with it. But because I believe the answer, at least for most of us, emerges from some of the theological considerations which have occupied us in previous chapters, it seems right to face it here.

Let it be noted that the question is "to read or not to read?" It is *not* "to write or not to write?" It may be assumed that in the study, in the preparation of the sermon, there has been the discipline of writing and often re-writing. Bishop A. F. Winnington-Ingram used to tell his ordinands that they should write all their sermons for the first twenty years of their ministry. It was good advice. It is recorded of J. H. Newman that he wrote his sermons three times, since he was often dissatisfied with the first two drafts. A leading Free Church minister of the last generation has told us that he built his style on his waste-paper basket. Writing not only disciplines style, compelling the writer to prune the cumbrous sentence and to muscularize the flabby phrase. It disciplines the preacher's logic, and forces him to ask himself whether there is *sequence* to the points which he is making, whether he is keeping resolutely to the central aim of the sermon. Writing disciplines the preacher's theology—many a heresy has been aired from the pulpit because it has never stared its perpetrator in the face from a

manuscript in his study. Writing compels the preacher to
come to terms with the time element. For lack of it, all too
many sermons have no terminal facilities, and remind the
listener of Christopher Robin's "dear little dormouse"
whose "eyes are small, but *his tail is e-nor-mouse*".

No: we are not discussing whether there should be care-
ful preparatory writing work. We are assuming that. We
are a stage farther on. We are thinking of the preacher
as he stands in the pulpit in his parish church. We are not
concerned with the unusual sermon preached to a university
or before a learned society. Such sermons may well call for
special methods as they call for special kinds of utterances.
We are thinking of vicar or curate face to face with the
people to whom he has been ministering during the week.
Is it best to have the results of the week's homiletical work
there, more or less in full, in front of the preacher, so that
he reads a manuscript (with varying success in his attempts
to hide from his congregation that he *is* reading)?

Let it be said at once that there are some who can read
their sermons, and who let it be *seen* that they are reading
them, and who yet hold the attention of their people.
Bishop Phillips Brooks was one such. His biographer tells
us (*Life & Letters of Phillips Brooks*, by Alexander V. G.
Allen (2 vols., Macmillan & Co. Ltd., 1900), Vol. II,
p. 20) that he not only read every word, but that he read
at great speed and at considerable length—and his people
hung on every syllable. I venture to think that there are
very few Phillips Brooks! There are those who are en-
dowed with photographic memories. Though they have
their full manuscript in front of them, they use it scarcely
at all, for they see it in their mind's eye though they do not
look at it. Happy men! Most of us have not that gift. There
are others who virtually learn their sermons by heart—a
course of action very unwise for most men, imposing on
them, as it necessarily must, an almost intolerable strain.

Strangely enough, we have quoted Bishop Phillips Brooks as an instance—a comparatively rare instance—of a man who could obviously read his sermon word for word without detracting from the power of the spoken word. It was he who defined preaching as "the communication of truth by man to men". We ventured to criticize that definition because of its inadequacy (*supra*, p. 24). But the chapter in which that definition occurs is valuable for the emphasis which it puts on the personality of the preacher (Phillips Brooks, *Essays in Preaching*, Chapter 1). Of that subject we have seen more in Chapter Six (*supra*, pp. 71ff.). It is an essential and vital part of preaching. St. John Baptist may describe himself as nothing more than the *voice* of one crying in the wilderness; but even a voice is a very personal thing, carrying many of the traits of the speaker's individual personality. *It is of immense importance that nothing should obstruct the personality of the preacher when he is at his work.* Anything which does that is greatly to be deprecated and, almost at all costs, to be avoided. *Is it not true that in nine cases out of ten a full manuscript does just that?* It comes between preacher and people, interrupting the give and take, the I–thou relationship, the sense of free *rapport* which must exist between them if the word of God is to reach the people uninterruptedly.

The point is of such importance as to allow of brief elaboration. It may be doubted whether any man can really *preach* over the radio. He can deliver an address, even with conviction and passion. But, however good a broadcaster he may be, the wireless cannot help being an obstructive element between preacher and listener. It serves as an effective block to much of his personality. Even television has a similar, if smaller, evil effect on preaching. True, the preacher can be seen as well as heard—an important part of the obstruction is thus done away. But in preaching there should be *traffic* between preacher and congregation, and the traffic should be two-way. Eye should meet eye; personality respond to personality; there must be give and take. For the preacher is not the only actor in the great work of preaching. If our argument in the last chapter is true, there is almost as much activity going on in the pew as in the pulpit, when God the Holy Spirit uses a man as His agent in the ministry of the word. People give to preacher as well as preacher giving to people; and both preacher and people give their joint offering to Almighty God.

A young man beginning to preach would be well advised never to become so tied to his manuscript that he cannot break free from it. And older men who have become accustomed to the security of a full manuscript might do well to break away before the tyranny becomes too strong, and to launch out into the deep in a new reliance on the Holy Spirit.

There is another point which merits consideration. Before we enter the pulpit we kneel down to ask the special help of God for our task. We put ourselves at His disposal in a special way for the ensuing minutes. We have done our preparation in dependance on His guidance. Now we are on the alert as we deliver what we believe and trust is His message. It may well be that, in the course of delivering the sermon, some illustration may occur, some little aside, which is in very truth the result of the action of the Holy Spirit on our mind. Is there not a grave danger that if we are tied too closely to our manuscript we shall fear to leave it sufficiently to allow of incorporating into the sermon that illustration or that fresh insight?

The mention of the word enthusiasm arouses a variety of reactions in people. But if George Herbert was right, as undoubtedly he was, when he said that there were "two things in Sermons, the one Informing, the other Inflaming" (*The Country Parson*, from Chapter XXI—"The Parson

Catechizing''), it can hardly be denied that there will be no
''inflaming'' if the heart of the preacher is not itself aflame.
But how often that is conspicuous by its absence. We are
chary of enthusiasm because we falsely equate it with
emotionalism. But enthusiasm, passion, urgency (call it
what you will) is an essential ingredient in all great preaching. ''As I listen to sermons''—I quote from Professor
Leonard Hodgson (*The Doctrine of the Trinity* (Croall Lectures 1942–43, Nisbet & Co.), p. 181)—''I am impressed
by the fact that over and over again preaching fails in its
effectiveness not because of defects in the preparation of the
subject-matter but because the preacher is not putting his
whole self into the delivery of his message. One recognizes
that the material is good, well and carefully thought out and
put together. But it fails to catch fire and kindle answering
sparks in the congregation because its utterance gives the
impression of being the performance of a routine duty.''
How often one has shared the Professor's impression! Why
should it be? Why is one so rarely reminded of Bunyan's
Evangelist, who ''was as though he pleaded with men''?
Is it sometimes because we lose the perspectives of eternity
in our preaching, narrowing our horizons too much to *this*
life, and failing to teach men how to die as well as how to
live? Is it because the *compassion* of Christ has never over-
mastered us? Is it because a manuscript blocks the flow of
our passion, and damps the fires of our enthusiasm? How
often does the sheer excitement of New Testament
Christianity, the thrill and magnificence of the Gospel,
break through from preacher to people if between him and
them there is a manuscript to be read?

Have I overstated my case, in my attempt to get my point
across? Perhaps so. It matters little, if some are led to re-
think the problem in their own instance. But to break a
lance with those who hold tenaciously to their full manuscript, and to do nothing more, would be to lay oneself

open to the accusation of writing a merely negative warning. Can nothing more positive be said? I believe it can.

It is not possible to lay down a law universally applicable to all preachers—"this thou shalt take into the pulpit, no more, no less". There can be no regimentation. Our homiletical gifts differ as clearly as our facial appearance, our finger-prints, our characters differ from those of our neighbour; and our preaching methods must therefore differ also. But it may be permissible for one who realizes, all too painfully, that he "has not already attained" and most certainly "is not already perfect" in this most demanding craft of preaching to outline certain courses of action which have been of help to him and so may prove of help to others. I believe that if, in a general way, some such method is followed, it may prove unnecessary to take into the pulpit a full manuscript with all the dangers which I have suggested as being inherent in that action. For the sake of clarity, I enumerate, though it is obvious that the order of the points may vary with the preparation of different sermons:

(i) The text or passage of Scripture having been decided on, it is of fundamental importance to study the context. A text or passage of Scripture is not just a convenient peg on which to hang our discourse. Indeed, a text out of its context is merely a pretext. The very etymology of the word "text", coming as it does from the Latin *texere*, to weave, shows that it is part of the warp and woof of a passage or a book, and should be part of the warp and woof of the sermon. We must not do despite to the section of Scripture which has provided us with our text.

Many are the stories of preachers who have forgotten this elementary lesson. One of the most pointed concerns the Bishop who said to the curate: "Young man, what did you preach on last Sunday?" *Curate:* "On 'hear the Church',

my Lord.'' *Bishop:* ''But there is no such text in the Bible.''
Curate: ''Excuse me, sir, but there is—'if he neglect to
hear the church, let him be unto thee as an heathen man . . .' ''
Bishop: ''Very well, then, I will give you a text for next
Sunday—'hang all the law and the prophets'.''

(ii) The next stage in the preparation of the sermon is to
live with the text which has been chosen. Live with it,
mull over it in your mind; centre your prayers on it; take
it for walks with you as you go visiting; take it to bed with
you so that, during the hours of the night, the sub-conscious
processes of your mind may be at work on it. Thus it will
become part of you. Was not some such process as this in
the mind of the Biblical writers when they spoke of eating
a roll of a book (*e.g.*, Ezekiel 2^9–3^4 and Revelation 10^{8-11}),
''inwardly digesting'' the divine message before giving
utterance to it?

Lady Lilian Adam Smith, in her delightful Life of George
Adam Smith, gives an account of the making of his sermons
in the early days at Aberdeen long before he became Professor and College Principal. There is a passage which is
germane to our present point (*George Adam Smith: A Personal
Memoir & Family Chronicle* (Hodder & Stoughton, 1943),
pp. 39–40):

''Early in each week he started thinking about a subject
and a text for the next Sunday. It would be 'simmering in
his mind' throughout the week, and on Friday or Saturday
he would shut himself up in his study to write. Often on
Saturday evening he would say, 'My sermon is just wooden,'
and he would throw it in the fire and start to re-write it,
perhaps from a different angle, or with some fresh inner
light that had come to him; often it was not finished till the
small hours of Sunday morning. Then it was delivered red-
hot with an earnestness which struck deep into the hearts
and minds of his hearers. His imaginative genius, his power

of depicting persons, places and events gave a vividness to each subject that he touched and made it live. No wonder that fifty years later he was described by one who remembered those sermons as 'the glowing young Evangel who drew us to Queen's Cross Church, which he crowded to the door with congregations more eager than any I have ever seen, before or since'."

(iii) The third stage is to find out what others have said about the theme chosen for the sermon. The *third* stage, not the second; for it is important to do one's own work on the subject before checking up with the authorities. If one may reverently say so, the Interpreter Spirit, the Holy Scriptures and a man of God intent to understand and expound are a great trio. Anything may happen when that trio meets. Only after that divine–human encounter over the Word of God has taken place should the preacher turn to his books. Then what wealth awaits him! He is indeed "the heir of the ages". He is not a lonely pioneer at his task. Others have been at it before him, men whose knowledge of God, of life, of theology, of a dozen branches of learning which bear on the Christian revelation is far greater and richer than his own. What they have written is part of his heritage. Gradually, as his ministry goes on, he enriches his collection of their works in his own little library; and constantly he is in and out of the public library of his nearest town, gleaning, culling, adding to his poverty from the amassed riches of the Church of Christ. As he reads, he may find that he has been on the wrong track in certain of his musings. His reading will serve not only to enlarge the horizons of his thinking but to correct his errors and reduce his ignorance.

(iv) While these preliminary disciplines have been going on, the preacher will have been jotting down notes. They will have been in haphazard order; anything which he thinks may be relevant goes down, a reference here, an illustration there. It is a good idea to use several sheets of paper some-times. If it appears, for example, that the sermon may take the shape of introduction, two points and conclusion, then four sheets may be used, one for each section. Then out of the primal chaos order will begin to emerge. Here the material is thin—more reading and thought will be called for. There the material is over-weighted—there must be a jettisoning of some of the cargo, or the ship will ride heavily or even sink. (How often—to change the metaphor —our picture is spoilt because we over-crowd our canvas.) Here there is lack of illustration or over-use of difficult terminology which makes the sermon like a cake with too much fruit and too little baking-powder. There the opening fails to arrest, or the ending to end! So the good work goes on, the craftsman employing all the skills known to him in hammering out something not too unworthy of the Lord for whom he works.

(v) Then comes the stage of writing out more fully. Of this I have written at the beginning of this chapter, describing this stage in the creation of the sermon as a discipline of style, of logic, of theology, of the time-element. But what comes next if, as has been suggested, it is in most cases the course of wisdom not to take the full manuscript into the pulpit? There comes the stage of reducing the sermon on to one small sheet, and of writing (or typing) these notes in such a way that a quick glance shows the preacher where he has got to and what comes next. A quick glance, for he must not be compelled to lower his head so that he cannot be heard, as he reaches the critical points in the sermon where one section ends and another begins.

If there are two places in the sermon which call for more care than others, they are the beginning and the ending. The *beginning*—for in the opening sixty seconds we largely win or lose our case. If we can arouse the interest of our hearers *then*, if we can draw to the pulpit the thoughts which are wandering in a thousand different directions, we are well on the way to holding our people's attention for the next twenty minutes. If we fail to interest and to grip in the first minute, it may take many minutes and much labour to pull back the wild horses which we have allowed to run away. The *ending*—for this is the climax of all our work, when the will of Mansoul is assaulted for the Master. At this critical point we often fail, our laziness or our sheer tiredness overcoming our sense of duty in preparation. Much excellent preaching work is spoilt by an ending badly prepared, and much harvesting is thus thrown away. A quick résumé, a recapitulation of our headings, a clinching of the whole sermon in a few, a very few sentences, and then have done with it. Leave the Holy Spirit to do His work, and remember that He has better opportunity to do so in silence than in the hurry of a garbled ascription.

IX

CHRISTIAN PROPHECY—A STUDY IN
1 CORINTHIANS 14

MUCH has been written by New Testament scholars on the
meaning of "prophecy" in the Epistles and on the function
of the New Testament "prophets". This is not the place
to enter into the question in detail. We may be content
with Professor H. L. Goudge's brief definition of it in his
comment (*Westminster Commentary* (Methuen & Co., 1927),
p. 111) on 1 Corinthians 12[10]—"*prophecy*, *i.e.*, inspired
preaching". He continues: "This was the gift of the
Christian prophets. . . . It might in some cases include the
power to foretell the future . . ., but primarily, as with the
prophets of the Old Testament, it was a gift for teaching
and exhortation." So again (*op. cit.*, p. xxxvi): "We speak
of Father Ignatius today as a great mission preacher—a
'prophet' or 'evangelist' St. Paul would have said. . . ." In
similar vein Professor H. M. Gwatkin notes (*Hastings'
Dictionary of the Bible*, Vol. IV, p. 127) that in the New
Testament the word "prophet" "keeps its general sense of
an interpreter of God's message". And C. K. Barrett
writes (*The Epistle to the Romans* (Black's New Testament
Commentaries, 1957), p. 238) of New Testament prophecy
that "like Old Testament prophecy it was primarily an
immediate communication of God's word to His people,
through human lips". It is to be noted that J. B. Phillips,
in his translation of the New Testament Epistles (*Letters to
Young Churches*, Geoffrey Bles, 1947), renders the noun
"prophecy" by the word "preaching" (for example,
Romans 12[6], "If our gift is preaching, let us preach to the
limit of our vision"), or the verb "prophesy" by "preach"

(for example, 1 Corinthians 14³, "He who preaches the word of God").

On this, then, as the fundamental characteristic of New Testament prophecy there would seem to be pretty general agreement—inspired preaching (Goudge); interpretation of God's message (Gwatkin); immediate communication of God's word to His people (Barrett); preaching the word of God (Phillips). And there is general agreement on the fact that the element of prediction, though not entirely absent and though "impressive to the vulgar" (cf. Gwatkin in *H.D.B.*, *ibid*.), is a very minor element in New Testament prophecy.

This is in line with, and is a legitimate development of, the best and highest strand in Old Testament prophecy. There is a paragraph in Dr. John Skinner's *Prophecy and Religion (Studies in the Life of Jeremiah* (Cambridge University Press, 1940), pp. 195–6) which is of such importance that it must be quoted as showing the rich soil out of which New Testament prophecy grew. "Jeremiah is conscious of standing in a personal relation to God, which we may call confidential, and of which the false prophets can have no experience. . . . He has stood in the council of Yahwe, has heard his word, has been sent by Him. His whole conscious life is pervaded by this conviction, which has come to him at the moment of his call—that before his birth he had been predestined and consecrated to the mission of a prophet. It is this which gives him the assurance that the truth which he perceives . . . is a revelation of the mind and will of Yahwe. This immediate consciousness of having the mind of God is the ultimate secret of true prophetic inspiration, which, being incommunicable, can neither be analysed nor applied as an objective criterion of an alleged revelation. It is strictly analogous to the experience of religious certainty in general—the *testimonium internum Spiritus Sancti*, 'bearing witness with our spirits that we are children of

God'. He who has it knows that he has it, though he who lacks it may be deceived in thinking he has it; just as a man who is awake may be sure he is not dreaming, whereas a man in a dream may readily fancy himself awake." This tremendous experience of the Old Testament prophets at their best is taken over and raised to a yet higher plane by the cycle of events which reached their climax on the Day of Pentecost.

Against that background we may come to a consideration of the fourteenth chapter of the first Epistle to the Corinthians. This chapter cannot be considered in isolation from the two chapters which precede it. Indeed, the chapter divisions are highly artificial and are unfortunate in that they tend to break up the continuity of a passage which runs unbroken from 12¹ to the end of chapter 14. The general theme is the gifts which God has given to His Church in rich profusion—the word of wisdom, of knowledge, faith, gifts of healing, prophecy and so on. Though the gifts differ widely in their variety and expression, it is the same Spirit who works through them for the benefit and enrichment of His Church. So much for chapter 12. Chapter 13 is devoted to that indispensible gift "without which whosoever liveth is counted dead" before God. This is to be "pursued" (14¹) as the greatest and most-to-be-coveted gift even of the trio of faith and hope and love.

In chapter 14 a contrast is drawn between the gift of tongues and prophecy. The former is not to be despised ("I would that ye all spake with tongues", v. 5; "I thank my God, I speak with tongues more than ye all", v. 18). But it may be surmised from what we know of the Corinthians and of their particular temptations and inclinations that they favoured the showy, the noisy, the ecstatic rather than the more sober and essentially ethical gifts of the Spirit. There is no doubt on which side St. Paul would have come down if a choice had to be made between the gift of tongues and prophecy. He stressed that the test above all others which the Corinthians must apply when considering the gifts of the Spirit was the answer to the question: "Is the Church being built up by the use of this gift?" "The speaker in a 'tongue' builds up his own soul, but the preacher builds up the Church of God" (v. 4, J. B. Phillips' rendering). That is the essential difference. "If the sounds of the speaker's voice mean nothing to me I am a foreigner to him, and he is a foreigner to me" (v. 11, Phillips). Tongues without interpretation are useless so far as the growth of the Church is concerned. *And*—an additional point to be noted, to which we shall recur later—they make no use of nor demand on the intellectual faculties of the speaker (vv. 14–20); and that, by itself, is sub-Christian. By contrast, prophecy, or, as we should say, inspired preaching, is intelligible to others (vv. 3 and 24–25), and makes full demands on the speaker's intelligence and intellectual powers (vv. 19–20).

We are now in a position to see precisely what are the purposes and effects of preaching as they are depicted in this chapter. There are two sections of special interest and significance, the first being v. 3 (with which we may compare v. 31), the second vv. 24 and 25.

(i) *Verse 3*—"He that prophesieth speaketh unto men to *edification*, and *exhortation*, and *comfort*." Here are clearly outlined three purposes of inspired preaching, which, while to a certain extent overlapping with one another, bring into focus certain indispensable elements of "prophecy".

(a) "*Edification*". The word is a favourite in St. Paul's vocabulary. That is not to be wondered at, for he was essentially a man of the city and delighted to use city metaphors. It calls for little comment, for we are familiar with the Pauline concepts of the Church as a building (note especially Ephesians 2¹⁹⁻²²) and as the Body of Christ (Romans 12, 1 Corinthians 12 and Ephesians 4). The building is being "fitly framed together" (Ephesians 2²¹), the Body is being "fitly joined together" (Ephesians 4¹⁶—the word is the same in each case); and preaching is one of the implements used by the Spirit in that process.

(b) *"Exhortation"*. The word *paraclesis* is so rich and full as to allow of no one English word as its equivalent. It often carries with it a note of comfort in sorrow. A classic passage in this connection is 2 Corinthians 1. It may be doubted whether this is the predominant meaning here, for the *third* word in the series in this verse deals with that element in Christian preaching. *Paraclesis* in the New Testament often conveys the idea of exhortation, and of stimulation. Indeed, it is most probable that there is a large element of this in the cognate word *Paracletos*, which the author of the Fourth Gospel uses of the Holy Spirit. He is not only the Comforter, even in the sense of Strengthener. He is the One who stimulates to fresh outbursts of mental and spiritual advance in the members of the Body. That may well be the meaning of *paraclesis* in this passage. It is the function of preaching to *stab awake* the conscience, to *incite* the mind, to *stimulate*, to *excite*. So St. Paul writes in v. 31, "Ye may all prophecy one by one, that all may learn and all may be *incited*." Professor R. H. Fuller gets close to this idea when he defines *paraclesis* as "a renewal and deepening of the apprehension of the *Kerygma* in the already converted" (*What is Liturgical Preaching?*, p. 22).

(c) *"Comfort"*. Here quite definitely is the note of consolation in grief, of encouragement in time of depression or distress. Not the least part of the Messianic programme which Jesus outlined at the beginning of His public ministry (St. Luke 4¹⁸, ¹⁹) was the healing of the broken-hearted. No one who broadcasts at all regularly in the religious programmes of the B.B.C. will be surprised at this, for the post-bag which is the outcome of every broadcast gives ample evidence of the heart-breaks which are the lot of great multitudes of people. One of the most important tasks of the Christian preacher is to bring the deep *comfort* of the Christian Gospel to those in sore need of it. It is more blessed to comfort the broken-hearted than to scold those present for the sins of those absent!

(ii) *Verses 24 and 25*—"If all prophesy, and there come in one that believeth not, or one unlearned—

(*a*) he is convinced of all;
(*b*) he is judged of all;
(*c*) the secrets of his heart are made manifest;
(*d*) falling down on his face he will worship God; and
(*e*) will report that God is in you of a truth."

It is not difficult to recapture the picture which St. Paul gives us in such vivid colours here—the assembled congregation, the ministry of preaching in process and the entry of one who is not a regular member of the Church. He may be an unbeliever (*apistos*), a Jew or a Gentile who has never before heard the Gospel or at least has never surrendered to the Christian allegiance. Or he may be "one unlearned"—(*idiotes*)—so the Authorized Version. The word probably refers to one who is not a member of the Christian congregation, not a fully fledged Christian, but at the same time not an "unbeliever". We may think of him as a kind of proselyte or catechumen (I follow here the interpretation of this verse given in *A Greek–English Lexicon of the New Testament and Other Early Christian Literature*, by W. F. Arndt and F. W. Gingrich (Cambridge University Press, 1957), *s.v.* ἰδιώτης). He enters. He comes under the influence of Christian preaching. The power of the Holy Spirit working through the prophetic ministry of the Church bears in upon him. He is never the same man again. Conscience is assaulted. "He is convicted and challenged . . . his secrets are exposed" (Phillips). It is not long before conviction leads to action and he is down on his knees worshipping. He is no longer half-way between the unbelievers and the Christian community. He sees that if he is to find God he will find Him *there*—in the Christian congregation. He is no longer a halting proselyte. He is ready to come in. Such is the effect of preaching—worshipping adoration and full membership of Christ's Body.

"He is convicted and challenged." Not many months ago I was travelling from New York to London by air. One of my fellow-travellers was a South African business-man. "Do you know the Bishop of Johannesburg?" he asked me. He went on: "He is a good man, but I do wish he would keep out of politics." The world would love to have it so, a Church with a message unrelated to burning moral and ethical issues, comfortably detached from life as it is. Readers of the Life of William Temple (by F. A. Iremonger (Oxford University Press, 1948), opposite p. 577) will recall the reprint of Low's cartoon which depicts the Primate standing on ground marked "Economic Fields" and opposite him the irate figure of Colonel Blimp pointing to a notice "Trespassers will be prosecuted". But the Bishop of Johannesburg and Archbishop Temple are in the line of the prophets of the Old Testament and of the New, in so far as they relate their message to burning moral and ethical problems of the day. Christian men and women have the right to look to the preacher for guidance on the rights and wrongs of moral questions; and the Christian preacher has the right and the duty to "convict" and to "challenge" his hearers. Writing of the seer of the Old Testament, Dr. E. G. Selwyn says (*The First Epistle of St.*

Peter (Macmillan & Co., 1946), p. 260) that "he had a reputation for practical insight which made his counsel sought for by many in regard both to public and to private affairs". And of the word *paraclesis* which, as we have seen above, is an integral part of preaching, he writes (*op. cit.*, p. 262) that "it signifies the moral strengthening which comes from the presence and guidance of those who are strong in the faith".

"Practical insight" and "moral strengthening"—these are integral parts of any preaching which is to tell in a world morally and ethically adrift. When St. Paul stands before Felix, he does not dissertate on religion unrelated to life. He speaks about righteousness, self-control and the coming of judgment—"the very subjects", as F. F. Bruce pointedly comments (*The Acts of the Apostles* (Tyndale Press, 1951), p. 427) "that Felix and Drusilla most needed to hear about". We have rightly reacted against the preaching of a merely "social Gospel"—rightly, that is to say, if by that phrase we mean a Gospel of self-effort divorced from the mighty acts of God in Christ and in the Holy Spirit. But where we find a church unconcerned with the grave social ills which surround it, a church with no social conscience, there we must ask whether the Gospel has been preached in all the fullness of its implications and whether it has been truly heard. St. Paul described the Gospel as "God's Word, a power in the lives of you who believe" (1 Thessalonians 2^{13}, Phillips). That precisely it is—a power working for righteousness personal and in the body corporate. It is the glory of the Church in South Africa to raise its voice against racial discrimination, which is contrary to the declared Mind of God. It is the shame of any church to remain silent and unmoved to action when it is surrounded by vice and crying social ills.

When, above, we spoke of *paraclesis*, we noted that stimulation of mind and conscience was an indispensable part of true preaching. St. Paul's main anxiety about "tongues" was that they called for no exercise of the *mind*. But prayer and singing (v. 15) and preaching (v. 19) all call for the use of the intellect to the glorifying of God and the building up of His Church. It must be so if all are to learn and to be stimulated and strengthened (v. 31). "A man cannot preach beyond his experience"—so it is often said. But is it true? Yes, if by that is meant that you cannot preach a Christ whom you do not know. No, if by that is meant that you confine your preaching to what you have yourself experienced of Him, for that would be to limit the riches of Christ and to impoverish your people. J. B. Phillips has an interesting rendering (or paraphrase) of Romans 12⁶, "If our gift is preaching, let us preach to the limit of our vision." It is our task to preach *beyond* the narrow limits of our personal experience, even to the limit of our vision. We catch a glimpse of the many-coloured wisdom of God reflected in the lives of His saints as recorded in the pages of the history of the Church or in some stimulating book of Christian theology. Very well, then: it is our task to point our people in the direction we have seen, though we ourselves may not have entered into this land of far distances. "Let us explore together"—this is the task of the preacher, as he bids his people join him on the pilgrim road.

H

X

A MISCELLANY AND A PRAYER

AND God said, Let there be light, and there was light.—
Genesis 1³

And Moses said unto the Lord, O my Lord, I am not
eloquent . . . but I am slow of speech, and of a slow tongue.
And the Lord said unto him, Who hath made man's mouth?
. . . Have not I, the Lord? Now therefore go, and I will be
with thy mouth, and teach thee what thou shalt say.—
Exodus 4¹⁰⁻¹²

By the word of the Lord were the heavens made, and all
the host of them by the breath of his mouth.—Psalm 33⁶

He sent his word and healed them; and they were saved
from their destruction.—Psalm 107²⁰

Then said I, Woe is me! for I am undone; because I am a
man of unclean lips. . . . Then flew one of the seraphims
unto me, having a live coal in his hand. . . . And he laid it
upon my mouth, and said, Lo, this hath touched thy lips;
and thine iniquity is taken away, and thy sin purged. Also I
heard the voice of the Lord, saying, Whom shall I send, and
who will go for us? Then said I, Here am I; send me. And
he said, Go, and tell this people . . .—Isaiah 6⁵⁻⁹

For as the rain cometh down, and the snow from heaven,
and returneth not thither, but watereth the earth, and
maketh it bring forth and bud, that it may give seed to the
sower, and bread to the eater: So shall my word be that
goeth forth out of my mouth; it shall not return unto me

void, but it shall accomplish that which I please, and it shall prosper in the thing whereto I sent it.—Isaiah $55^{10, 11}$

Is not my word like as a fire? saith the Lord; and like a hammer that breaketh the rock in pieces?—Jeremiah 23^{29}

Son of man, stand upon thy feet and I will speak with thee. . . . And he said unto me, Son of man, I send thee . . . —Ezekiel $2^{1, 3}$

O son of man, I have set thee a watchman unto the house of Israel; therefore thou shalt hear the word at my mouth, and warn them from me.—Ezekiel 33^7

I will stand upon my watch, and set me upon the tower, and will look forth to see what he will speak by me.— Habakkuk 2^1

The poor of the flock that waited upon me knew that it was the word of the Lord.—Zechariah 11^{11}

Jesus came . . . preaching.—St. Mark 1^{14}

To this end was I born, and for this cause came I into the world, that I should bear witness unto the truth.— St. John 18^{37}

All bare him witness, and wondered at the gracious words which proceeded out of his mouth.—St. Luke 4^{22}

The common people heard him gladly.—St. Mark 12^{37}

They went forth, and preached everywhere.—St. Mark 16^{20}

Paul was wholly absorbed with his preaching.—Acts 18^5

I have not shunned to declare unto you all the counsel of God.—Acts 20^{27}

Whosoever shall call upon the Name of the Lord shall be saved. How then shall they call on Him whom they have not believed? And how shall they believe in Him of whom they have not heard? And how shall they hear without a preacher? And how shall they preach except they be sent? —Romans 10$^{13-15}$

We preach Christ crucified.—1 Corinthians 1^{23}

Preach the word; be instant in season, out of season.— 2 Timothy 4^2

Holy men of God spake as they were moved by the Holy Ghost.—2 Peter 1^{21}

That which we have seen and heard declare we unto you. —1 John 1^3

> The lyf so short, the craft so long to lerne,
> Th' essay so hard, so sharp the conquering.
>
> Geoffrey Chaucer

> Lord, how can man preach thy eternal word?
>   He is a brittle little glass:
> Yet in Thy Temple thou dost him afford
>   This glorious and transcendant place
> To be a window, through thy grace.
>
> But where thou dost anneal in glasse thy storie,
>   Making thy life to shine within
> The Holy Preachers: then the light and glorie
>   More rev'rend grows, and more doth win;
> Which else shows waterish, bleak and thin.
>
> George Herbert

He was as though he pleaded with men.—John Bunyan

Thou art a preacher of the Word; mind thy business.—
Old Puritan

God had only one Son, and He made him a preacher.—
Thomas Goodwin

A man must not only know what to say; he must have a
vehement longing to say it.—Walter Bagehot

You cannot drop the big themes and create great saints.—
J. H. Jowett

You are preparing a sermon. The spiritual and intellectual atmosphere hangs like a dull leaden cloud over you.
It is a wearisome, almost loathsome struggle to advance at
all. What then shall you do? Will you yield to your
temptation, give up the struggle, and take an old sermon,
or go on and set down any commonplaces that may come
into your head, so as to fill so much paper or occupy so
much time? No, you will take the nobler alternative; you
will, by God's help, wrench the best out of yourself,
whatever effort it may cost of self-concentration or self-
loathing. And what is the result? Believe it: this is the
result of experience. It is just this one sermon, which has
caused you so much dissatisfaction, which has touched some
heart. Others which have flowed smoothly from your pen
or your lips, have glanced ineffectively off the ears or the
minds of your hearers. But of *this*, thank God, you can say
that it has moved one soul . . . And why was this? Because
it cost you so much.—J. B. Lightfoot

It takes a good deal of a man to make much of a preacher.
—A. T. Robertson

It is into the Bible world of the eternal redemption, that
the preacher must bring his people. The only preaching

which is up to date for every time is the preaching of this
eternity, which is opened to us in the Bible alone—the
eternal of holy love, grace and redemption, the eternal and
immutable morality of saving grace for our indelible sin.—
P. T. Forsyth

No true preaching of the Cross can be other than part of
the action of the Cross. If a man preach let him preach as
the Oracle of God, let him preach as Christ did, *whose true
pulpit was His Cross*, whose Cross made disciples apostles,
in whose Cross God first preached to the world, whose
preaching from the Cross has done for the world what all
His discourses—even His discourses—failed to do. . . .
Every true sermon, therefore, is a sacramental time and
act. It is God's Gospel act reasserting itself in detail. The
preacher's word, when he preaches the Gospel and not only
delivers a sermon, is an effective deed, charged with blessing
or judgment.—P. T. Forsyth

Preaching . . . is the Gospel prolonging and declaring
itself.—P. T. Forsyth

Of all the actions of the Christian Ministry preaching is
the highest, and the test of our reverence for our profession
is our performance of the preacher's duty.—Hensley
Henson

The Church's preaching is the Word of God in a derivative and tertiary sense. It is derived from the secondary
sense, the Bible, which, in its turn, is derived from the
primary sense, Jesus Christ.—R. H. Fuller

Preaching the Word is God's ordinance; but if it be not
His Word, but human notions and inventions that are

preached, it ceases to be an ordinance of God.——Edward Bickersteth

To me preaching was a necessity of my being. I felt it as something wonderful that I was allowed to address a congregation every Sunday about the deepest questions of life.——A. Schweitzer

The preacher is the man whose calling it is to create forms out of the most precious material which this world provides. His material is the everlasting Gospel, his tools are his full powers of thought and imagination, his object is to create a form which shall be the best possible to convey to other minds and imaginations the glory and beauty of that which he is seeking to portray.——F. W. Dillistone

> Easy to bear
> The lack of praise
> When walking in the world's secluded ways;
> But should men smile
> And flatterers bring
> Their gift of honeyed words, their incense swing,
> Not easy then to scorn the keen delight;
> Often have I been wounded in that fight.
> Safer the lowly pew,
> The preacher's chair how perilous, how few
> Fit for their Master's cause
> Too pleased with men's applause:
> So while I teach I tremble, lest I win
> Praise that shall quench the fire of Truth within.
>   John Searle

Lord Jesu, teach Thou me that I may teach them. Sanctify and enable all my powers, that in their full strength they may deliver Thy message reverently, readily, faithfully, and fruitfully. O make Thy Word a swift word, passing from the ear to the heart, from the heart to the life and conversation: that as thy rain returns not empty, so neither may Thy Word, but accomplish that for which it is given. O Lord, hear! O Lord, forgive! O Lord, hearken and do so for Thy blessed Son's sake.——George Herbert

INDEX OF NAMES

INDEX TO BIBLICAL REFERENCES